Svengali,
or the orchestra called
GILL EVANS

Raymond Horricks

Selected discography
by Tony Middleton

Spellmount
TUNBRIDGE WELLS

Hippocrene Books
NEW YORK

First published in UK in 1984 by
SPELLMOUNT LTD
12 Dene Way, Speldhurst,
Tunbridge Wells, Kent TN3 ONX

ISBN 0 946771 40 4

Horricks, Raymond
Gil Evans.—(The Jazz masters)
1. Evans, Gil   2. Jazz musicians—Canada—
Biography
I. Title   II. Series
785.42'092'4   ML419 E9/

First published in USA in 1984 by
HIPPOCRENE BOOKS INC
171 Madison Avenue
New York, NY 10016

ISBN 0 88254 909 X

Series editor: John Latimer Smith
Cover design: Peter Theodosiou

Printed & bound in Great Britain
by Anchor/Brendon Ltd, Tiptree, Essex

for Grizelda *and* Alan Garner

Illustrations

Cover: Gil Evans, London 1983 (Tim Motion)

Title verso: Gil Evans, London, 1983 (Tim Motion)

Title Page: Gil Evans, London, 1983 (Tim Motion)

Recording 'Miles Ahead', 1957 (Courtesy of CBS Records, photo: Don Huntstein)

With Miles Davis, 1958, during the recording session for 'Porgy and Bess' (Courtesy of CBS Records, photo: Vernon Smith)

At the time of his 'New Bottle, Old Wine' LP with Cannonball Adderley (Max Jones)

In Copenhagen, 1974 (Jan Persson)

Backstage at the R.F.M., London, 1983 (Tim Motion)

At the Royal Festival Hall, London, 1983 (Tim Motion)

Conducting his British Orchestra, 1983 (Tim Motion)

With the author, 1983 (Tim Motion)

A volunteer, you assign yourself specific roles and risks according to your judgement of their brilliance and importance, and you see when life itself may be justifiably devoted to them.

MICHEL DE MONTAIGNE
'Of Experience', *Essays (1588)*

Svengali is actually an anagram based upon the letters of Gil Evans' own name. It was first spotted and applied by his friend and fellow-orchestrator Gerry Mulligan – and is particularly apt when considering the players, over a long period of time, Gil has presented via his writing: from Miles Davis and Julian 'Cannonball' Adderley to George Adams, to Marvin 'Hannibal' Peterson. However, although apt it doesn't really say enough. Because what one feels compelled to add is that Gil has been, still is, the most outstanding arranger of jazz outside of Duke Ellington; and in an active life his *corpus* of finished work has never contained a *cliché*.

The man probes, he creates, and his inherent curiosity has made of his art a challenge, a lover, an autobiography and – overall – a logical fulfilment . . .

Jazz music, in common with Gil Evans himself, has been exclusive to this, our present century. There were many antecedents, of course: melodic and harmonic in Europe, rhythmic in Africa. And there is a molehill of a case that Buddy Bolden, a New Orleans barber and cornet player, blew the first hesitant notes of jazz ahead of the year 1900. But the fact remains. What we call the real jazz has been performed in the 20th century only.

In accepting this, we are confronted by a further fact. Jazz has moved along faster than any other known development in the history of music. It has grown, expanded, changed, been subject to upheaval and revolution, absorbed that revolution and progressed again, suffered bouts of anarchy . . . but still survived. All within the space of two and a half generations.

The problem of writing a brief book about jazz and the orchestra called Gil Evans – illustrated with certain records – lies in tempering therefore one's beliefs, natural prejudice and true enjoyment with the necessary objectivity. While knowing that beneath such an approach there are twin-traps: a purely Narcissistic selection or a fistful of historical dust.

Fortunately there are stabilizers. Stabilizers, and some preliminary aids against the dark. For as one's critical boat rocks in the music's shifting seas, so there is an awareness of powerful improvisation on the port side, fine orchestration to starboard and feelings of genuine swing propulsion down in the engine-room. Also, to begin with, beckoning, you have the glowing

11

beacons of Jelly-Roll Morton and Louis Armstrong. Then a lighthouse: Charlie Parker. In between are vital buoys, sounding in turn: Earl Hines, Don Redman, Bix Beiderbecke, Jack Teagarden, Roy Eldridge and Lester Young. Beyond are lights along the harbour-wall (Dizzy, Thelonious, Clifford Brown, Rollins, Eric Dolphy). All there to guide you safely through the cleared channel. Around the headland, but not that far away, is the wide bay of Duke Ellington; and nearby the other one of Count Basie – with its mooring facilities for individual craft. So: for your present purposes you can steer by them, directly towards the last of the lights: fairly sure the musician it represents will not elude you. Again, you know that Gil Evans marks a deep-water anchorage with lots and lots of space; which in turn presupposes the future of jazz.

'When in doubt choose greatness,' Cyril Connolly once wrote. Well, in jazz this would mean greatness in soloists, in composition, in arrangement. Because it is precisely the great figures in jazz who are most clearly linked together. They forge their own musical chain; or rather they unwind a continuous thread of determined exploration through the congested labyrinths of accelerating evolution. The original explorers become in their turn guardians. But the unwinding doesn't stop here; the sense of adventure is never lost. Like Henry the Navigator on his outcrop at Sagres the guardians have amassed stores of knowledge, they provide the cerebral finance and offer encouragement to younger captains sailing for uncharted waters. As this writer steers for the harbour in search of Gil Evans, so new musicians are already weighing anchor. 'The true voyagers are those who go for the sake of travelling . . . and who, balloon-like, never shrink from their destiny. Without quite knowing why, they say, Let us depart!' (Baudelaire).

Tell the story of all these great ones, explorers and guardians and more explorers – and there you have the history of jazz. Just find the men. The music goes with them.

How to be sure of greatness though?

Well, one is fortunate yet again; the jazz century has coincided with the age of the gramophone. Enough evidence is permanently preserved in grooves or on tape for us to be able to worry out the truth. Play the records. Play them often. Then arrange your men in sequences, with their performances around them. A kind of fresco gradually emerges. Certain areas across its surface remain obstinately obscure. You drop a few names, even one or two 'acknowledged giants' – and suddenly the area in question becomes clear: the detail, the pattern and, of course, its associations with surrounding areas. Everything is there. Eventually in this way the whole fresco is restored to you. It stays in your own possession; but you will show it to others, or try to, and you should be capable now of explaining things about it.

The names of the musicians I have mentioned so far were not selected at random. For Gil Evans in musical terms has the same kind of head as the Roman god Janus. He is looking back at the same time as looking forward. He will be using Jelly Roll Morton's *King Porter Stomp* over and over, continuing to analyse it, recreating it in entirely new ways. He knows where the roots lie; and how to draw sustenance from them. ('I take possession of the old world – I inhale it – I appropriate it.' – *Henry James*).

Likewise there is his individuality. He has put together sounds with combinations of instruments which for decades the academic colleges have told us just won't work. Gil Evans has made them work. His music is a tapestry of difference and excitement – and incorporates everything that the man has picked up during his life and thought good. Some years ago, asked about his direct influences, he replied, 'Everything I've ever heard. The good *and the bad*. With the bad being especially important because it teaches you what to avoid. But it isn't just music. As a boy it was the sounds in the street, police sirens, all of that.' Which perhaps when considered isn't all that far removed from the birdsong, Hindu rhythms and microtonal music and dynamics we are told have inspired the compositions of Olivier Messiaen. The one big difference however being that Gil has opted to free himself of his various creations largely through the equally free individualities of other men. His orchestra is never just a relay station . . .

Which brings us to 1984. Probably an appropriate time to be evaluating Gil Evans, for George Orwell's year has a prophetic, even a cautionary ring for most of us. Where afterwards will we be? What then will we be doing? Will we even *be*?

Gil is no longer a young man; except in ideas. But he has now come out from behind the soloists his music once acted as an accompaniment for, choosing to travel his inventiveness as the leader of other, talented musicians all around the world: from Japan to Sydney, to London and on to Germany.

Another thing, with the physical passing of Ellington the responsibility placed upon Gil Evans – himself in his later years – is awesome. And yet, happily for jazz, he is more than up to it; a man with his cherished devices, but who always manages to produce the *new*. That we should have been made to wait until February 25, 1978, when he was sixty-six, before being allowed to hear his orchestra 'live' in London seems little short of musical criminality. But his Festival Hall concert alone was worth the wait. A kind of jazz equivalent to the Antal Dorati/ Royal Philharmonic Orchestra's 'Beethoven' cycle of the same period, or maybe in a 'pop' sense the Rita Coolidge/ Kristofferson concert at the Royal Albert Hall just a few months later. Also, together with his recent recordings, it afforded us a marvellous opportunity to gauge what Gil is currently reaching out towards.

The magnificence of the Gil Evans orchestra itself goes almost without saying. He is always an intuitive picker of the right men for the job; and then he makes use of their every potential. At the Festival Hall concert there were only thirteen players including himself, but the writing often featured five trumpets or flugelhorns (both the tuba and French horn players doubled), while the variety of rhythm was sometimes bewildering, with trumpeter Marvin 'Hannibal' Peterson banging away at the tubular bells and nearly everyone else playing something or other. Gil played concert grand, electric piano and a hand-held percussion box. And he didn't utter a word from beginning to end. He had walked on at the start, wearing a Burgundy-coloured corduroy suit, a wad of parts under his arm, looked up once at the house, adjusted his spectacles and then it was time to play. The music was left to speak for itself. But in the face of a standing ovation when it was over he permitted himself a delighted smile and the gesture of clasped hands. He was in accord with his audience. He knew the concert had gone well.

In fact the personnel of this later orchestra had been recruited from wildly disparate sources: Gil's belief being that talent, ultimately, must out. Altoist Dave Sanborn is an ex-Paul Butterfield and Stevie Wonder man who also now plays the sopranino and lyricon; George Adams, tenor and other reeds, once worked with Lightning Hopkins and Howlin' Wolf Burnett as well as in the Mingus Workshop and more recently with Don Pullen; while the show-stopping trumpeter Marvin Peterson (Gil's Cat Anderson) came from a background of Chuck Jackson and T-Bone Walker. He has an emotional range and brilliance quite unique in jazz. Another featured trumpeter, Lew Soloff, is ex-Blood, Sweat & Tears, and lead-trumpet Ernie Royal – 'the iron man' – was the best of his kind on the New York session scene. Tuba-player Bob Stewart, like Howard Johnson before him, has elevated the scope and treatment of his instrument to unprecedented heights; while Gil has come upon a remarkable organist from Japan, Masabumi Kikuchi. However, all of these musicians have seemed fully reconciled to Gil's latest writing and the way, based on simple thematic ideas, or just *motifs*, it has brought a new spontaneity to his already very flexible designs for the jazz orchestra.

When they take the stand these men are not always certain who will take the solos on the different numbers they play. 'I always liked the idea of spontaneously getting up to play,' is how Gil explains it (although he himself kept his abilities as a pianist under wraps until past the age of forty). 'On a job anybody can play, and they usually do. I try to think of music in which everybody has some way of expressing himself. That's why we play a lot of *heads* now. Sometimes something will come from that; everybody will start filling in around it and maybe veer off in some way – and all of a sudden I have an improvised arrangement.' Nearly the same impression is created by several of the tracks from his recent recording sessions.

Here, therefore, we have yet another circular movement, which again harks back to the earliest jazz. Which in turn makes sense of his band playing new arrangements of pieces like *King Porter Stomp* and Leadbelly's *Ella Speed*.

Meanwhile the leader himself remains restless; but with the necessary self-confidence to go on and revolutionize even the

music in heaven given the chance. Other musical developments continue to be brought in. The familiar brooding atmosphere and rich harmonies which accompany Marvin Peterson's *Zee Zee*. The exhilarating shouts of unison brass on the latest version of *King Porter* and the delicate use of mutes in different places. These special Evans' characteristics are now joined by his delving into the potentialities of electric keyboards, synthesizers and the bass guitar, and in ways which leave other orchestrators at present working with jazz materials open-mouthed. Rhythmically too, with a series of pulse-beats that take their beginning from Gil's intimate knowledge of Elvin Jones' versatile, polyrhythmic drumming, but then going on to involve further elements: like the juxtaposition of unusual time-signatures, making the feeling appear at the same moment very complicated and disarmingly simple, and drawing into the rhythm section tonal sounds from many different parts of the world. Alongside all of which there is an increased cross-fertilization of thematic ideas, with the jazz now derived from such additional sources as Billy Harper's earth cries and the tunes of the doomed, drug-haunted pop guitarist, Jimi Hendrix.

Where to next with this most fascinating of living musicians? Only one thing is certain: it promises to be an absorbing journey. For he has gradually moved away from his earlier prevailing formalism to a breathtaking use of his musicians' inner judgements and his own capacity to go, musically, where no one else in jazz so far has dared. *Svengali*? Yes, still: because the man understands the musicians and the music is also the man . . .

Charles Fox is a good source to quote on certain aspects of the earlier Evans. Bearing in mind that at this particular period Gil was much more consciously ornate than he is today; and again that his then reputation rested largely upon the brilliance and the surprises of his orchestral supports for the solos of trumpeter Miles Davis, newly become a jazz 'superstar'. The Evans orchestra itself, with its equivalent, but different brilliance and often amazing freedoms was still some way around the timescale of a musical corner. Although – and such is the creative cohesion of the man – Evans formal and Evans free are always instantly recognisable as being a similar combination of intelligence and imagination as say, at one stage removed from the human mind, causes twinned Rolls-Royce engines to work. Often he has been neglected or underemployed; but nothing has succeeded in fouling his great mental installation. Its motors have continued to turn over.

'The Miles Davis Capitol sessions, the last of which actually took place in 1950,' he (Charles Fox) writes*, '. . . .ushered in a new era of small-group jazz, bringing to the music a fresh sound and a much more ambitious conception of texture. And as well as using trumpet, trombone, alto and baritone saxes, piano, bass and drums, the band included a French horn and a tuba; it was the first time that these two instruments had been incorporated within a specifically jazz group, although for some years they had been exploited very skilfully by the arrangers with Claude Thornhill's orchestra, one of the most interesting dance bands of the 1940s. The link with Thornhill's band is significant, for not only were several of the musicians taking part in the Capitol sessions members or ex-members of that orchestra but the Miles Davis band had been planned at a series of meetings held in the apartment of Gil Evans, Thornhill's chief arranger.

'At the time Evans was thirty-six, a surprisingly mature age for a man just about to revolutionize jazz orchestration, although in no other art-form would it seem at all odd. In a way it was typical of Evans that he should have remained so stubbornly in the background before producing this *tour de force*. The same thing was to happen again between 1950 and 1957, the years which preceded his score for the 'Miles Ahead' LP, when Evans worked at many tasks – act music, vaudeville, night-clubs, as well as orchestrating for radio and TV. He also occupied his time reading musical history, biographies of composers and music criticism and listening to records; he was filling in, as he put it later, *the gaps in my musical development*, gaps which sprang from the fact, the surprising fact, that he had never received a proper musical education. *I've always learned through practical work*, he says. *I started in music with a little band*

* 'Jazzmen Of Our Time', ed. Raymond Horricks, London, 1959.

that could play the music as soon as I'd write it. This empirical method has been shared by at least two other distinguished jazz composers – Duke Ellington and Tadd Dameron. They, along with Evans, can boast like so many of the pioneers of jazz, that no academicians ever defined for them what was possible and what was impossible.'

However, Gil makes a clear distinction between Ellington and himself. 'There never has been, there isn't, and there never will be another Duke,' he insists. 'I love him, his men and his music madly, I owe them plenty, but I go my own way. And incidentally, not *too* much emphasis should be placed on my being self-taught. Anyone who ever gave me a moment of beauty, significance, excitement has been a teacher. I have made a partial list. It's enormous, but I'll mail it on request!'

He was born in Toronto, Canada – on May 13, 1912 – although both his parents were Australian. He was christened Ian Ernest Gilmore Green (but later took the surname of his stepfather). When he was eight the family moved to Spokane in Washington State, then in turn to Idaho, Montana, Oregon and finally Stockton, a town about 70 miles from San Francisco. His stepfather was a miner and just had to go where there was work. In Stockton he first heard jazz music over the radio. And already he was becoming obsessed by sounds. 'When I was a kid I could tell what kind of a car was coming with my back turned,' he recalls. Later he could recognise the sounds of Louis Armstrong, Jack Teagarden, McKinney's Cotton Pickers and Benny Goodman without their needing any announcements. As regards classical music, he went first to the French Impressionists and then into Russian music. 'And I picked up everything I could of Bach's. People can devote their whole lives to Bach. It's a fantastic adventure. So is Chopin, but Bach especially'.

In 1933 he formed his own local band in Stockton and wrote every one of the arrangements. In 1936/37 he put together a similar band to work at The Rendezvous Ballroom by Balboa Beach. He was showing some talent in addition as a pianist by this time, but preferred to concentrate on orchestration. 'So I had Buddy Cole playing piano for me. And later on Stan Kenton. In truth, because I never did have any what you'd call proper lessons I just had to work things out by myself. It had started, really when I was around some kids who could play. Then I started copying things off records. The first one was Red Nichols' *Ida, Sweet As Apple Cider*. It's a great record. I can hear it in my mind still. It's beautiful, very slow and with Adrian Rollini playing the lead on baritone-sax: the man who first inspired Harry Carney.'

In 1938 the band began to be fronted by vocalist Skinnay Ennis, and as such landed a job with Bob Hope's radio show. At which point Claude Thornhill was hired as an additional arranger. Gil and he got on immediately. They swapped ideas, and when Thornhill left to form his own band, Gil says he 'haunted Claude' until the latter took him on.

'It was essentially a French horn band,' Gil emphasises. 'Trumpets and trombones would play in derby-hats to avoid vibrato.' Meanwhile the French horns were blended with the brass and reeds to produce a variety of new tone colours. 'A characteristic voicing for the Thornhill band,' he goes on 'was a French horn lead, one and sometimes two French horns playing in unison or a duet . . . the clarinet doubled the melody, also playing lead. Below were two altos, a tenor and a baritone or two altos and two tenors. The reed section sometimes went very low with the saxes, being forced to play in a sub-tone and very soft.' All of the saxes were at the same time capable clarinet players, and later, in 1947, after Thornhill had been in the U.S. Navy and Gil in the Army they added Bill Barber on tuba, not playing in the old, New Orleans rhythmic style but again being blended into the ensemble.

'He (Claude) wrote in a very peculiar style. It was all his own. He'd have high clarinets voiced over the brass for tunes like *Pizzicato Polka*, *Liebestraum* and *My Heart And Thy Sweet Voice*. His arrangements could be stunning. Very different though. I mean, unison clarinets, all five of them way up there, imitating violins. There was one number called *Portrait Of A Guinea Farm*. His own composition, his own piano playing. It's a fascinating number. It's a gimmicky title, of course. I never thought of it as being a literal programme title. But the music's a real experience, great.'

'Then there's his *Snowfall*, which was originally called

Fountains In Havana. Again there were the five high clarinets, with the double melody on the bottom of the four-part harmony, and the five brass playing like a pentatonic scale underneath. Like G flat, A flat, B flat, D flat, E flat, or even F – the whole scale, almost, clustered up close together underneath those clarinets playing the melody. That was so characteristic of Claude, and his original creation. After a while it became part of my own timbre box.'

Gil delighted in the richness and depth of these ensemble voicings: as revealed by his scores of *Loverman, Polka Dots And Moonbeams* and *There's A Small Hotel*. Also though he had become equally fascinated by the musical devices of be-bop, and he now set about adapting the fast and exceedingly tricky chord sequences of this new form of small-group jazz to the bigger band: hence the Thornhill recordings of *Anthropology, Donna Lee, Yardbird Suite* and *Sorta Kinda*. 'I did more or less match up with the sounds of people like Lester Young, Charlie Parker and Dizzy Gillespie,' he says of the period. 'It was their rhythmic and harmonic revolution which was influencing me.' He even shared a room for several weeks with Charlie Parker. However, when converting such music into use by larger forces he admits that 'an interdependence of modern thought and its expression was necessary. Because if you express new thoughts and ideas in old ways then you take the vigour and excitement out of the new thoughts.'

No less a personage than Thelonious Sphere Monk pronounced this particular Thornhill group 'the only really good big band I've heard in years!' And some promising young soloists had joined; the most notable being altoist Lee Konitz. It was unfortunate, therefore, that the bandleader himself remained sceptical about be-bop – pointing out that their slower, softer pieces like *Snowfall* were proving the more popular with audiences. Eventually he opted for a much more stark, almost a sombre sound, and Gil grew frustrated. He still liked Thornhill personally, but as he states, 'Everything – melody, harmony, rhythm – was moving at a minimum speed. The sound hung like a cloud. If it had been possible I think Claude would have had the band hold a chord for a hundred bars.'

And so he left. Which in turn left him free to join with Miles Davis, Gerry Milligan, Johnny Carisi and John Lewis in creating what has been termed in jazz 'the birth of the cool'. It wasn't really all that cool. But it introduced a thoughtful complexity of sound and a more linear approach to the music after several years of very angular be-bop themes . . .

A lot depended on Miles Davis himself, of course: who had been working hard at his technique – and also on what amounted to a completely different jazz trumpet-style. For although retaining a good deal of intensity, he now decided to seek a new tone. Which in turn led to a smaller, tighter sound at fast *tempi*, usually achieved with mutes; and a severe loneliness when playing ballads. It seemed to confirm his natural lyricism though. And again to fit with his improvising across the traditional breaks and bar-lines: a way of allowing his improvised ideas greater continuity. He gives credit to the late Freddie Webster, a trumpeter with the Earl Hines and Jimmie Lunceford bands, for providing certain clues. Essentially though the change of style was all his own – and as startling in contrast with the boiling volcanoes of Dizzy Gillespie and Fats Navarro as Bix Beiderbecke had appeared in deviating away from Louis Armstrong. Someone said that it sounded 'like a man walking on blue eggshells'. Other musicians dubbed it 'cool' – and in this way the further revolution brought about by Miles and Gil and Gerry Mulligan got its name.

'Miles had liked some of what Gerry and I had written for Claude,' is how Gil tells it. And consequently, when the trumpeter began to think in terms of expansion, of a new orchestral development, he was already aware of several harmonic affinities with the two arrangers. He entered into a series of discussions with them, and the outcome was the nine-piece band which opened at New York's Royal Roost in September 1948 and made the three historic recording dates for Capitol in the twelve months following.

'The instrumentation for the Miles sessions,' Gil stresses, 'was caused by the fact that this was the smallest number of instruments that could get the sound and still express all the harmonies that Thornhill had used.' But the six wind and three rhythm instruments still offered an exciting range of possibilities. For instance, 'if the trombone played a high second part to the trumpet,' he explains, 'there would be more intensity because he'd find it hard to play the notes. But you have to work these things out. I never know until I can hear it.'

He scored the thoughtful and introspective *Moon Dreams*, as well as *Why Do I Love You?* and *Darn That Dream* for the group's vocalist, Kenny Hagood. More importantly though he created the startlingly original arrangement of Miles' own *Boplicity* – a theme written under the pseudonym of 'Cleo Henry' – and hailed by French critic André Hodeir as being 'enough to make Gil Evans qualify as one of jazz's greatest arranger/composers'.

Boplicity is quite remarkable for its harmonic daring ('an interpenetration of instrumentation and harmony' – Hodeir). Also for the way it guides the shape and structure of what could be a solo invented by Charlie Parker through dramatic switches of voicing and instrumental colour. Again to quote Charles Fox, 'The textures constantly shift and unfold, while at the same time there is a remarkable atmosphere of relaxation about the performance, despite the care and precision which have gone into it. There is too a breakaway from the rigid structure still obsessing jazz in the way Evans made the last phrase of his theme spill over into the following chorus, and, during the second chorus, in the way he spread the first part of the bridge over six bars (instead of four). But it is the texture of this performance which is probably its most satisfying aspect, the way in which each eight bars of the final chorus is scored for a different instrumentation, the way in which the French horn is used to create a dissonant effect, a dissonance arising from timbre rather than harmony . . .'

Financially, and also in public, Miles' band of 1948/49 was a disaster. Audiences at the Royal Roost were used to all the excitements of Dizzy Gillespie's big band by this time; and to the popularising of be-bop by other, lesser men. They failed to understand Miles' new concept and he closed after only two weeks, never to appear again in public with this kind of ensemble. But gradually, via its handful of records, the band came to have a profound and lasting influence upon modern jazz. Its careful reconciliation of so much that was fresh and stimulating about the be-bop revolution with collective exploration and imaginative scoring represented a point of no return.

As individuals the associate members went on to seek out future kingdoms. Miles disappeared to brood on the subject of a post-Parker quintet, then reappeared with the finest small group of the late '50s and 1960s. Lee Konitz, the most important soloist after Miles, drifted back into his association with Lennie Tristano and perfected the lineaments of his alto-saxophone style. A truer interpretation of the word 'cool'. Gerry Mulligan took himself and his formidable abilities to California, becoming the leader of a piano-less quartet there. Johnny Carisi has had his non-jazz works performed by chamber groups in many different parts of the United States.

As for Gil, he simply went back 'down into the street' again: to listen, to learn, to let his 'think-tank' refill. But meanwhile quietly preparing himself for what was to become (with Ellington's) the most important jazz orchestration of the next twenty years. And fully justifying his contention that 'orchestration is one of the elements of composition. You might say that it is the choice of sound units and their manipulation as part of expressing a musical idea.'

Talent does whatever it wants to do. Genius does only what it can.
DELACROIX

Not that Gil didn't keep himself busy until 1957 and the making of the LP 'Miles Ahead'. He did an enormous amount of commercial writing that was always meticulous and above all highly professional. But at the same time it caused many people to fear that for purely financial reasons he was now well lost to jazz. What only a few close colleagues knew was that alongside this mass of popular accompaniments Gil continued to function mentally on another, quite separate musical level: gearing his background and accumulated knowledge and inherent creativity for the next big leap forward.

27

I will try to summarize his writing of the next seven years as briefly as possible. Because although important in that it gave Gil his living, it only occasionally touches upon his story as a jazz musician. He did play a little piano with Gerry Mulligan at Basin Street and in a duo with drummer Nick Stabulas in another club in Greenwich Village. Otherwise though it was all studio work: TV, radio and recordings. He wrote for Pearl Bailey, Tony Bennett, Polly Bergen, Peggy Lee, Johnny Mathis, Helen Merrill and Lucy Reed. Plus an unhappy session for Charlie Parker backed by the Dave Lambert Singers. With Lambert writing the vocal parts and Gil the accompanying orchestral ones, and Parker sick again; well, it just didn't work out. In fact a (somewhat) better date was one he did for vibes-player Teddy Charles and where the format allowed him to be much more his natural self. Even so, for me the recorded results lack an overall emotional spark. No matter. He did a good job in penning frames for the various singers – and all the while the vital process of a fresh musical germination and its subsequent interior growth was continuing unabated . . .

If the birth of the cool records for Capitol brought about a quiet, secondary revolution within modern jazz, then the issue by CBS of the LP 'Miles Ahead' came upon the scene like a bomb going off. Not long before this Gil had been talking to Nat Hentoff of *Down Beat* magazine. 'There were some sections on records I'd done,' he said, 'that I liked – but I didn't like any of them as entities. I'm still developing my personal sense of form. Until recently I hadn't done much composing of originals because the paths I follow hadn't led towards it. I was interested in the language. I did a good bit of work. Maybe sixteen bars in a *pop* song: I'd take my own chorus, so to speak. And I would always stay pretty close to the melodic line.'

But perhaps such words were a jazz equivalent of first-night nerves. For when copies of 'Miles Ahead' reached reviewers and the shops the consensus of admiration was unanimous. As the great Dizzy Gillespie complained, 'I wore out my first one inside three weeks, so I went round to Miles and said *Give me another copy of that damn record!* Everyone should own it.' Another respected figure, Bill Matthieu wrote: 'The mind reels at the intricacy of his (Gil Evans') orchestration and developmental techniques. His scores are so careful, so formally well-constructed, so mindful of tradition that you feel the originals should be preserved under glass in a Florentine museum.'

'Miles Ahead' is indeed the kind of jazz record that happens only once in a long time, like Louis Armstrong's *West End Blues* or Parker's *Now's The Time*. That it occurred in the same year as Ellington's 'Such Sweet Thunder' and within twelve months of Lester Young's final flourish on 'Jazz Giants '56' is therefore a source of wonder, a definite *Annus Mirabilis*.

Apparently the basic conception for the album was Miles' own, but stemming from the musical association he'd formed with Gil in the days of his ill-fated 1948/49 nine-piecer. Miles: 'Yes, he (Gil) definitely is the best. I haven't heard anything that knocks me out as consistently as he does since I first heard Charlie Parker.' To which Gerry Mulligan has added, 'Gil is the one arranger I've ever played who can really notate a thing the way a soloist would blow it.' Which was precisely how Miles wanted these new arrangements to be. For he would take the only solos, playing flugelhorn, and in front of the biggest band he had ever worked with: nineteen men in all.

Anyway, their various discussions led to a framework by Gil of ten pieces, each a mini-concerto, but also linked to the one which follows, so that a continuous and overall portrait emerges of Davis the mature soloist. 'He (Miles) confirms what we already knew about him in that he is the most lyrical of modern jazzmen. But whereas the lyricism of Charlie Parker, in his great moments, seemed to want to burst open the gates of delirium, Miles' lyricism tends rather towards a discovery of ecstasy. This is particularly noticeable in slow numbers, where Evans' lyricism is even more closely tied up with Davis'.' (André Hodeir). Meanwhile too the flugelhorn gave a more mellow, rounded edge to the soloist's tone.

Hodeir finally points out the perfection of those written-out passages in which Miles' horn is used to lead the ensemble. But other, equally impressive features of Gil Evans also come out in the writing. His dismissing the conventional saxophone section, for example, in favour of one mixing saxophones with woodwind. And his obvious delight in having the collective trumpets play fast figures which have all the intricacy of early

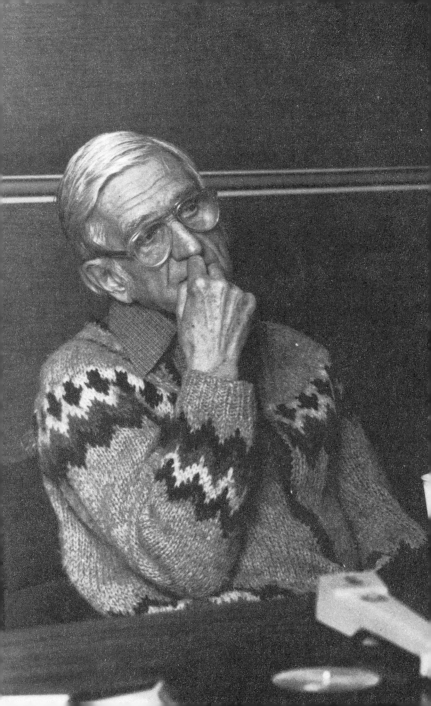

be-bop solos. Then there is his deliberate extending and enriching of the tonal sound, from the rooted depths of the tuba to the tree-tops of the other brasses and the flutes. And again his juxtaposed time-signatures. In parts of Delibes' *The Maids Of Cadiz* he has the bass in 2/4 while the drummer, Art Taylor, plays 4/4, and often through the LP Miles plays 3/4 against the orchestra's 4.

As regards form, texturing and orchestral techniques I can only mention isolated finds. For here as well one becomes aware of deliberate contrasts added to the agreeable links. The brilliant brass outbursts during Johnny Carisi's *Springsville* seem to emphasize the delicately harmonized effects of the slower *Maids Of Cadiz* which follows. Just as the defined ensembling and Rabelaisian use of tuba in Dave Brubeck's *The Duke* throw into relief the constantly shifting patterns of Kurt Weill's *My Ship* which follows that. *Miles Ahead* (an Evans original) is almost entirely ensembled and in its spurning of accepted breaks and bar-lines recalls Gil's earlier *Boplicity* score for Miles. *Blues For Pablo* is even more unusual, for it develops a creative conflict between the Spanish-type minor theme and a blues theme in the major, the first time this had been attempted in jazz. The short riff of Ahmed Jamal's *New Rhumba* is frequently varied in presentation; nevertheless it reveals to us Gil's growing interest in brief, strong melodies as the basis for improvisation instead of often over-tricky chord sequences and is a very sophisticated return to primitive roots. *The Memory Of The Blues* is again a thoroughly harmonized piece, while J.J. Johnson's *Lament* features both semitone progressions and whole tone ones. *I Don't Wanna Be Kissed* is a concerted swinger and ends the LP with an Ellingtonish flourish . . .

Following the critical acclaim accorded 'Miles Ahead', there were to be three subsequent collaborations with Miles and a group of similar size on record, plus the 'live' taping of a Carnegie Hall concert in 1961 – when pianist Wynton Kelly nearly carried off the solo honours.

A fresh approach to George Gershwin's 'Porgy And Bess' revealed another new development in Gil's writing. 'When he wrote the arrangement of *I Loves You Porgy*,' Miles noted, 'he just put down a scale for me. No chords . . . which gives you a lot more freedom and space to hear things. I've been listening to Khachaturian carefully for six months now and the thing that intrigues me are all those different scales *he* uses. All chords, after all, are relative to scales and certain chords make certain scales. You go this way, you can go on forever. You don't have to worry about changes and you can do more with the line. It becomes a challenge to see how melodically inventive you are. When you're based on chords, you know at the end of 32 bars that the chords have run out and there's nothing to do but repeat what you've just done – with variations. I think a movement in jazz is beginning away from the conventional strings of chords, and a return to emphasis on melodic rather than harmonic variation . . . with fewer chords but infinite possibilities as to what to do with them.'

The LP 'Quiet Nights' is a collection largely devoted to the exploration of bossa-nova rhythms; but it does go off at a tangent to include a magnificent ballad rendition by Miles of Michel Legrand's *Once Upon A Summertime*, as well as Gil's adding a harp to his instrumentation. However, and applying a more analytical perspective here, although at the time the record went into the 'best-seller' charts, overall it has not lived on in people's minds to the same extent as the 'Sketches Of Spain' album made in 1959 and '60. But then it doesn't contain the remarkable rescoring of the middle movement from Joaquin Rodrigo's *Concierto De Aranjuez*; another amazing achievement even by Evans' high standards. Bill Matthieu again concerning 'Sketches': 'This record is one of the most important musical triumphs that our century has yet produced. It brings together under the same aegis two realms that in the past have often worked against one another – the world of the heart and the world of the mind . . . what is involved here is the unison of ideas with emotion, precomposition with improvisation, discipline with spontaneity.'

Miles proved to be at his most sensitive and intuitive through the *Concierto*. While Gil remained typically modest afterwards, his only comment being: 'I've always inclined to Spanish music, but I didn't really absorb it from the Spanish. I got it from the French Impressionists first – and then from Spanish Impressionists like De Falla.'

33

What is interesting in addition from the 'Sketches' sessions is that at last we are allowed a few glimpses of Evans actually working: because sleeve-note writer Nat Hentoff was given the okay to be present on every occasion. John Williams, now famous as the composer of soundtrack music for 'Star Wars' and 'Close Encounters Of The Third Kind', told me many years ago that a Gil Evans' session always appears to start in chaos; with the arranger moving about, explaining things to individual players and only rehearsing little bits of each score. But then, suddenly, all the different parts begin to come together and the music emerges as something to arouse wonderment.

At the 'Sketches' recordings Gil, aged forty-seven, reminded Nat Hentoff of 'a lean, greying diplomat who collects rare species of fern at weekends. Though always polite, he is in firm control . . . and insists on hearing exactly what he has written.' For the *Concierto*, 'Miles had joined Gil at the spare piano and they started discussing Miles' part which was spread out, accordion-fashion, over many sheets of manuscript paper.' Then, 'Miles went into the control-booth, remarking *I always manage to put my foot in it. I always manage to try something I can't do!*'

'The take began with Miles sitting on a stool; a trio of trumpet, trombone and flute behind him; and Gil directing in the centre of the orchestra. He (Evans) conducts with an almost ballet-like flow of motion. He uses both arms, and keeps the beat going like a Poseidon calming troublesome waves. He is extremely careful that all the dense textural details and marking of dynamics are performed precisely and are recorded so that all the interweaving parts emerge clearly. At one point later in the afternoon, he cut off one take and said into the microphone, *Are you getting a blending of the three flutes? I only hear one out here*. A & R-man Teo Macero assured Gil that all three were distinctly audible in the control-booth. Then Gil went into the booth, heard for himself and was satisfied.

'By four, the shape of the piece was becoming established. The characteristic, fiercely mournful Spanish melody (originally composed for guitar and orchestra: R.H.) was a strong one. Evans' sketch for Miles looked complex, but Miles seemed to have no difficulty improvising around it. The orchestra's function, as in other Evans' scores, was to provide partly a support for and partly a commentary on Davis' solo statements. The range of colours was extreme, and they changed often, sometimes subtly dissolving into slightly different shades and at other times breaking sharply from ominous cool to brighter blends. By means of more complete instrumentation and varied voicings, Evans gets an unusually full-bodied sound for jazz. *These look like flute parts we're playing*, lead trumpeter Ernie Royal said during one break, shaking his head in respect and exasperation.

'The rhythms were complex and several of the musicians found it hard to keep their time straight. Gil stopped a take as the rhythms became tangled. *The tempo is going to go*, he waved his arm in an arc, first to the left and then to the right, *this way and that way. Just keep your own time and let the rhythm* go. He again made a slow even wave to further illustrate his point.

'In the control-booth, the visiting Hall Overton, a classical composer who has also been involved in jazz as a pianist and arranger, said, *This is the toughest notation I've ever seen in a jazz arrangement. It could have been written more easily for the players and the result would have been the same, but Gil has to have it the way it happens in the piece, I mean exactly. Fortunately, these guys are among the best readers in town.*

'For the rest of the afternoon, the takes continued to improve. On one, Miles began to play in the lower register with deep feeling and a fuller tone than is usual in his work. *Beautiful*, Macero said. *The writing there is almost Gregorian*, he turned to Overton. *It's all diatonic.*

'He asked Evans if the tympani came in too softly. *I wanted it to be just a whisper*, Gil replied, *just a little cushion of air, something to keep the thing floating. I think it's all right. The tuba is too loud though.*

'*That melody*, Miles was still marvelling at the piece, *is so strong that the softer you play it, the stronger it gets, and the stronger you play it the weaker it gets. Yes*, Gil said. *It's distilled melody. If you lay it on too hard, you don't have it.*

The attention focussed upon Evans as a result of his work with Miles led to his at last being able to make records under his own name. Initially these were still studio sessions, and again a summary becomes necessary. They vary from 'Gil Evans And Ten' which reveals the arranger adding bassoon to his tonal palette; to 'New Bottle, Old Wine', heavily featuring altoist Julian 'Cannonball' Adderley; to 'Great Jazz Standards' (with a superb, slow but powerful reinterpretation of John Lewis' *Django* included); to in 1963/64, 'The Individualism Of Gil Evans', when he used trombonist Jimmy Cleveland and tenor-player Wayne Shorter (borrowed from Miles' quintet) to great advantage.

All these LPs are clearly identified by Gil's previous approach to jazz writing: the search for tonally satisfying contrasts, the shifts of texture and so on. But in addition they mark his increased self-confidence as a pianist. From now on his groovy, blues-based keyboard style will be represented on every Evans record.

The collections also reaffirm that, in his quest for the new, he never neglects the importance of personal roots. W.C. Handy, Leadbelly, Jelly-Roll Morton, Louis Armstrong, Bix Beiderbecke, Don Redman, Fats Waller and Billie Holiday. Together with his modern colleagues, Lester Young, Thelonious Monk, Parker, Gillespie and Clifford Brown. Each of these has a composition re-examined in dazzling fashion within the Evans' canon. As well as some longstanding favourites by Irving Berlin, Cole Porter, Richard Rodgers and Kurt Weill.

Finally too there is more evidence of his impatience with fixed forms, and of his consequent return to very flexible melodic sources. Already he had pointed out to Miles Davis the advantages (meaning greater freedom) to be gained by ignoring certain bar-lines. He felt that improved phrases should determine the continuity of a solo and not just the bars. Which in turn left Miles dissatisfied with the 12- and 32-bar forms and would in time transform the musical growth of his quintet. So, the search by both men for the ways and the means of escape was definitely on. In Gil's case, gradually his own original compositions came to be essentially brief; sometimes just one phrase of melody with a few, strategically-placed chords. Yet herein, eventually, lay real strength, for they allow a soloist to develop his improvisation in a more elastic, and therefore far richer manner. And obviously with musicians of the calibre of Miles, 'Cannonball', Wayne Shorter and George Adams the potentiality becomes enormous: leading, in effect, to an open-ended, scalar playing where the form itself is simply allowed to grow (spontaneously) around a mood, a single motif and even the sounds of the group conceived in layers. Meanwhile Miles Davis would work towards a new leanness in his solos: playing far fewer notes, but investing each one played with its maximum significance.

The best musical documentation of how the Gil Evans mind was beginning to rejig the basic materials of jazz is contained on his 'Out Of The Cool' LP of 1960, an album which needs to be examined more closely than the others I have listed. Partly because of its inherent qualities: for it's a jazz 'classic' in the same exclusive mould as 'Miles Ahead' and 'Sketches Of Spain'. But also because, although made in a studio, it represents the first emergence of the Gil Evans Orchestra as we have since come to know it playing concerts and festivals.

Late in 1960 he took a band into The Jazz Gallery in New York City. After a number of experiments, this was the instrumentation he had decided to settle for, and with which he then recorded for Impulse, with Creed Taylor as producer. It consisted of two trumpets, three trombones (including a bass trombone), two alto-saxophones doubling flute and piccolo, tuba, himself on piano, electric guitar, acoustic bass and – of some added consequence – two percussionists: the ex-Dizzy Gillespie drummer, Charlie Persip and the even more remarkable Elvin Jones.

Of the outcome I'll begin by drawing what strikes me as a valid parallel, if an unusual one. I've always found reading Proust's 'Remembrance Of Things Past' is like entering a sacred and profane cathedral. Well, I think of Gil Evans' *La Nevada* track on his 'Out Of The Cool' LP in rather the same way. Wherever you put the needle down during this 15½-minute performance there is always something interesting happening, which can be enjoyed for itself or as part of the whole. And that whole is also a microcosm of the way Gil's later career in jazz has gradually taken on shape and purpose.

The fact that the band was working together in public helps to explain the impression of organization *and* spontaneity during *La Nevada*. The other reason is the theme itself: only four bars in length (and one Gil had used before), but strong in its simplicity and allowing for long solos with passages of improvised or 'head' arrangement developing behind them. The theme moves back and forth from G minor seventh to G major where it is actually notated, but stays in G minor for the solos.

This 'open' style of writing announces a definite departure from the more complete orchestration of 'Miles Ahead'. Also, there is a deliberate phasing out of inner texture so that the bass line more clearly complements the melody, which seems to make for increased virility. But while 'open', long and from the soloists' point of view more melodically 'free', Gil never actually loses his grip on the form. There are various internal climaxes with subsequent diminuendos – which in releasing the sound levels also relieves the emotional tension. In this way nothing ever appears forced or over-controlled, not even in the rhythm section, where the basic beat remains a constant factor throughout.

La Nevada opens with a solo piano figure from Gil. The rhythm instruments then enter separately, setting up an intense, medium-fast tempo: Gil uses maraccas to reinforce the drum part. The theme is first fragmented by muted trumpets and flute with guitar interjections; then afterwards stated directly by, in turn, piano, the three trombones and the trombones with muted trumpets and woodwind. All the soloists who follow play extremely well: Johnny Coles on trumpet, Tony Studd (the bass trombone), Budd Johnson – searingly – on tenor-sax, Ron Carter, the new bass sensation and Ray Crawford on guitar. But it is in the variety of what they play, and how Gil surrounds them, frequently using some of his rhythm instruments orchestrally, which reminds me so much of the varieties in Proust.

As usual he had prepared himself very thoroughly for the record, knew exactly where he could allow the music to go free and it had paid dividends. One cannot expect a masterpiece on every occasion of course; this I realise. Most creative people would settle for one or maybe, given a bit of luck as well, two or

Recording 'Miles Ahead', 1957

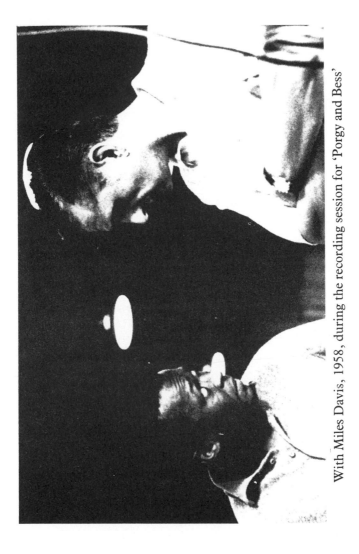

With Miles Davis, 1958, during the recording session for 'Porgy and Bess'

At the time of his 'New Bottle, Old Wine'
LP with Cannonball Adderley

In Copenhagen, 1974

Backstage at the R.F.M., London, 1983

46

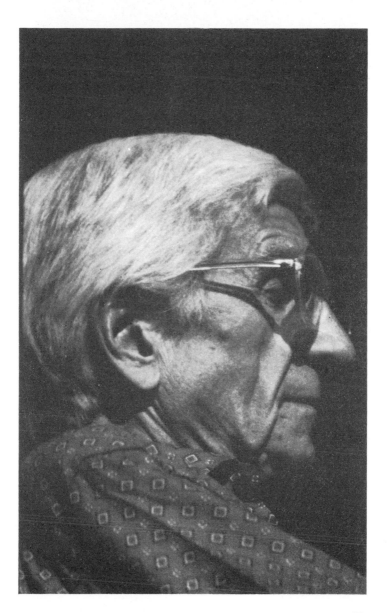

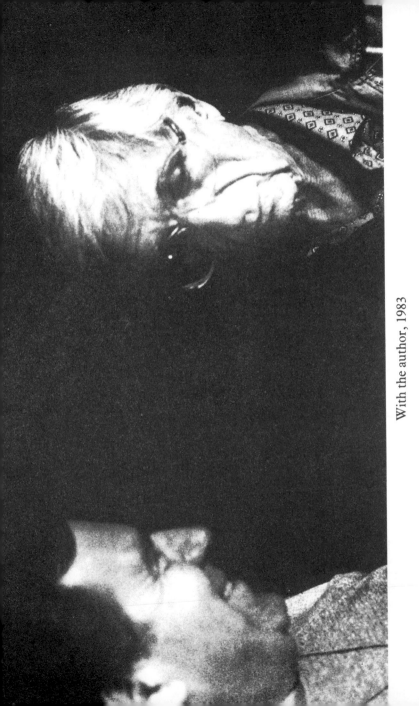

With the author, 1983

three in a lifetime. However, Gil has shaded somewhat ahead of that . . .

Following 'Out Of The Cool', another album under his name, 'Into The Hot' was released in 1962. But apart from donating his musicians, and being photographed for the LP-cover, Gil did not participate in any working sense. It was merely his way of sponsoring two other composers he admired: his friend from the Miles Davis Capitol sessions, Johnny Carisi, whose 'colossal unity' he speaks of; and pianist Cecil Taylor. Of the latter he has said: 'When I hear him I burst out laughing in pleasure because his work is so full of things. There's so *much* going on and he is such a wizard that whatever he does bristles with all kinds of possibilities.'

After this though, for Gil himself there came another period of retreat. 'For me, it was a question of a total life, a whole life, which has priority over any one of the things you do in the course of living. They are all part of it, but sometimes they have to wait a while. Emotional development for me is like that. If I feel the need for some emotional development, well, I think about music, and play, and even write. But as far as the product is concerned, there is no product.'

His life became nomadic, his work sporadic. In 1963 he collaborated with Miles Davis again on music for a play intended, eventually, to have been presented on Broadway, 'The Time Of The Barracuda'. They got the music taped, it was used during the show's San Francisco try-out – and then dropped after a union dispute over its use in Los Angeles. The play itself never reached Broadway and all we really know of the music is Gil's treatment of one theme, *Hotel Me*, included on 'The Individualism Of Gil Evans' LP.

He scored five out of nine tracks for Kenny Burrell's 'Guitar Forms' LP and wrote the accompaniments for Astrud Gilberto's 'Look To The Rainbow' collection. In 1966 he took bands to the Monterey and Pacific Jazz festivals, and in 1968 he received a Guggenheim Fellowship for composition. Otherwise he remained largely out of view, and of the public's ear. In the United States, even to this day he is still somewhat neglected, although idolized by jazz *aficionados* in Europe and Japan. As he told Les Tomkins of 'Crescendo International' in 1978: 'I'm not getting any new work in America now. So I came to Europe to pay the rent. And I meet lots of people who know about my records. It's nice to meet them.'

The revised, and perhaps definitive Gil Evans Orchestra finally surfaced in 1973 with the 'Svengali' LP issued by Atlantic. I say 'perhaps', and even that guardedly, because nothing ever is all that definitive with Gil except for his abilities. There are continuous changes of personnel within his groups and his writing itself is constantly undergoing re-examination and development. If Gil likes a new player, even a total unknown, he'll use him – or her. Likewise, if a new cultural experience appeals to him, somehow or other it'll get incorporated into his music-making.

However: what the 'Svengali' LP reveals, and is still true of the bands he takes out on tour and records with today is that music, jazz or otherwise, cannot be stationary. It has to keep evolving, experimenting, finding out what is there and if it is possible. Gil revels in personal, practical discoveries; and also in what is happening all around him. Consequently, on the 'Svengali' tracks one begins to hear post-Ornette Coleman and Eric Dolphy musicians. Players like the talented Billy Harper on tenor-saxophone, also Howard Johnson, who amazingly doubles tuba, baritone-sax and flugelhorn; plus a first, dynamic appearance by 'Hannibal' (Marvin Peterson).

Then there is the rhythmic legacy left by Elvin Jones, who had convinced Gil that the jazz beat can be divided up, conceived in terms of eight rather than four beats to the bar. Which in turn alters the continuity and flow. To go back to Charles Fox, 'Drumming like Jones' enables a soloist to hang in the air, like Nijinsky caught in mid-leap, or, more relevantly perhaps, like a soloist in Oriental music.'

The other 'key' event relayed by 'Svengali' is the leader's initial interest in electronic sounds: beyond just his earlier use of an amplified guitar. Through various sections of the record he plays electric piano, the bass (played by Herb Bushler) is also amplified and there is a full-time synthesizer expert employed, David Horowitz. But I must stress: these instruments are used on all occasions for their blending with, and genuine contributions to the overall patern of the music; never merely for effect. They fit *because they are made to fit*. On the other hand, Gil doesn't do anything by halves. In exploring for what is possible he can be as stubborn and relentless as his Taurus birth-sign suggests. Once content in his mind that these electrified keyboards had something good to offer, the only course open to him was signposted 'go on'. Which is why, by the time of his famous Festival Hall concert of 1978 he had added a mini-moog and Masabumi Kikuchi on electric organ, who also delighted departing fans by remaining on-stage after it was all over and showing them how Gil and he played the various hand-held percussion boxes. Also, Gil had acquired by this time Sue Evans (no relation), who plays tympani and most other classical percussion instruments as well as jazz drums.

As mentioned before, by 1978 the music had become increasingly free. But there was still a captain and a human being at the concert grand.

He had missed out on the planned collaboration with rock-guitarist Jimi Hendrix as a result of the latter's accidental and premature death. Although he had made up the lost ground by first of all presenting at Carnegie Hall, and then recording an album of Hendrix compositions. And from both before and since this album it has been rare for a Gil Evans Orchestra concert not to include at least one piece by Hendrix: be it *Angel, Crosstown Traffic, Foxey Lady, Little Wing,* the near-magical *Up From The Skies* and *Voodoo Chile.* At the Festival Hall we got *Angel* (featuring Dave Sanborn's alto) and one of the lesser-known, but no less potent Hendrix themes, *Stone Free.* Together with Gil's latest thoughts on Mingus, John Lewis and Charlie Parker. In between section passages and trumpet solos 'Hannibal' banged away at the tubular bells; while multi-reedman George Adams blew so long and so well in his featured solos that afterwards he had to go and crouch down in a yoga position to get his breath back. *Even so*: what a night!

As Dave Gelly has written, 'We all came reeling out of the hall after that February concert, none of us thinking we should ever be able to re-live the extraordinary musical experience of the past couple of hours. Gil's music had been almost too big to grasp. In every nook and cranny of the texture there was something vital going on, some tiny musical organism bursting into flower, while the vast sound of the whole thing engulfed us and carried us along. It is not often that one's highest expectations are surpassed. We looked forward to a treat and received instead a gift of incalculable value.'

'God knows,' he goes on, 'by what strange alchemy, he manages it. To watch him shuffling benignly about the stage you would think that everything was going on without reference to him at all. Masabumi Kikuchi seemed absorbed in his own thoughts, scrabbling in a random kind of way at the keyboard. But listen to the way his little phrases give depth to the piano figures, the drum pattern, the bass line at the opening of *Parabola* (on RCA LP PL25209 – R.H.). It *looked* accidental, it comes within a hair's breadth of being chaotic, but it isn't. It is superbly delicate and right. Without the vague-looking elderly gentleman in front it would very likely have degenerated into a shambles. His very presence seemed to bring order out of potential chaos . . .

'But, of course, it isn't all as mysterious as that. The structure of the pieces may be loose, but when the ensemble enters it is fearsomely accurate. With unerring instinct he has adopted elements from contemporary practice and used them for his own ends. The capacity of free jazz to surprise the listener with random juxtapositions fascinates him, but he sets these effects in a context of great precision. In rehearsal he will work painfully over four bars of orchestration while leaving great tracts to the inspiration of the moment. When the piece comes to be played though, those four bars emerge quite clearly as the cornerstone of the whole thing.'

And so he goes on into the 1980s, and his own seventies. With no diminishing of his creativity and obviously every willingness to travel his orchestra and to fill it with the best musicians available. 'I wanted to have fifteen men think and play the same way,' is how Count Basie once described *his* orchestra. Add the progress jazz itself has made since then, plus an orchestrator of originality and a touch of genius at the helm, and it becomes possible to understand what a Gil Evans appearance is all about . . .

To conclude, I want to let the man say some things himself. He rarely gives in-depth interviews. Not because he's temperamentally difficult or impolite. Simply on account of his being (usually) either too busy thinking about music or just as likely making it. But he was particularly forthcoming with Les Tomkins of 'Crescendo', and several statements by him in answer to the latter's questions will made a suitable addition to this profile.

Gil Evans speaks

The interview was conducted just before the 1978 Festival Hall concert; which Gil was clearly looking forward to.

L.T. *The line-up of this band is one, I suppose, that you try to keep to as much as possible whenever you do anything.*
'Yes, it's the same band – except that there's one change now. There are three trumpets instead of two and I have no trombone. I decided to try just a little shift in orchestration, eliminating the trombone and one French horn.'

L.T. *Also you have an organ instead of guitar. Is Masabumi Kikuchi using the guitar book?*
'He's using the guitar book, that's right. But what he's done – he took off my parts and copied them all over again for himself. At school in Japan they learn that calligraphy, and their lettering is so *fine*. When he copies the parts out, they're so small, but so legible. You can see them, but they're done with such a fine hand it really is amazing.

'Then I had to add the third trumpet book, and give some of the trombone parts to the third trumpet and some to the alto.'

L.T. *By now you must have a pretty big library to draw from.*
'Well . . . not all that big. We play Charlie Parker tunes – *Cheryl, Bird Feathers* and *Relaxin' At Camarillo*. We do those all in one tune. He wrote them all in C, so we just play a C blues, and we include those three heads. And we start out with the three-part fugue opening from John Lewis' *Concorde*. Then we'll play maybe *The Meaning Of The Blues* – George Adams plays that on tenor. It's the same arrangement I did for Miles Davis – except that it's somehow different. Possibly it's more flashy now!

L.T. *This is something you've always done over the years, really; isn't it? You revise arrangements, stretching them out in a different way – such as* Summertime *and* Where Flamingos Fly *(from the 'Out Of The Cool' LP – R.H.).*
'Right. In fact I did make another record of *Flamingos*, with Billy Harper, but it never got released. Gee, he plays great too –

I've got a tape of it at home . . . I played it only the other day. We made it on an album for Capitol, but just as we finished it a new administration came in and cancelled about twenty-five projects – and ours was one of them.'

L.T. *To jump back in time now . . . I've heard that for 'Miles Ahead' and 'Sketches Of Spain' you virtually closeted yourself away for long spells while you were working on some of those charts. Is this the way it is sometimes?*

'I've forgotten how long it took. A lot's happened since then. It's hard to remember. Sometimes it takes a long time to get the concept of the sound you want – you know, to get it in your mind. Or the pacing of the music. But once it's firmly in your mind it comes out very fast. On a project like that, you may run into a difficult time, but when you've finished one or two like that, then all of a sudden one'll come along, and you'll do it in five minutes. If you're into that, the whole thing is not a wonderment any more: you're committed to a certain sound. Although I'm not a fast writer, I don't deserve the notoriety for being as slow as I am, because my total product is small. But it's not because I'm slow to write it that it's so small. It's small for a number of reasons I guess – one of them being that because I wasn't raised around music a lot, I created my own musical world later. I don't have the game habit – I mean the musical games that are very important to a prolific writer; it's a compulsion, almost to do it. He'll say to himself: *Well, today I think I'll write something for* . . . and he'll name a combination. Then he'll sit down and write it for a combination like that, because he likes the challenge of that game – to *do* that thing. It may turn out to be a brilliant piece, and it may not, you know – but it's an interesting work, anyway. But I have not had that habit.

'Also, I've liked a lot of other things besides music. I've liked to be outdoors a lot, for example. Which I never get to be any more in New York, but I still like to be out in natural surroundings and I can use up a lot of time like that – which is very non-intellectual.'

L.T. *Have there been certain individuals you've admired and wanted to write for as featured soloist, but have not had the chance to do so?*

'Oh, I've had disappointments. One was Pres, Lester Young. We were working on the album. *Way Down Yonder In New Orleans* in A was one piece. But he didn't have time. He wanted to make the album, but he wanted to die more I guess. He came in from his home on Long Island, and decided to stay at the Alvin Hotel across from Birdland. He never ate a thing. Then he came back from Paris, got into the hotel-room again, and had a heart attack.

'Another was Louis Armstrong. I met him once, we talked for a while. He thought we ought to make an album. I'm a Louis Armstrong expert, you know; his records were the ones I learned music from. But on account of his manager, Joe Glaser, I didn't get the job. He said he'd never heard of me – although Louis had said he'd liked my Miles Davis things . . .

L.T. *Then another disappointment was Jimi Hendrix – you'd planned to do an album with him, hadn't you?*

'That's right. He was coming into town that following Monday. Alan Douglas had arranged for us to meet, he'd given him the 'Sketches Of Spain' album. And the idea was for him to make a guitar record – not to sing. Because Alan felt, as I felt too, he wasn't appreciated, even by himself.

'The way he died – it was just a tough break, to be careless enough to use barbiturates and alcohol. I mean it happened to Tommy Dorsey. Terrible.'

L.T. *But you did the next best thing and made the 'Gil Evans Plays Jimi Hendrix' album as your tribute to him.*

'Yeah – and RCA never did promote it. The man who is now President of Columbia even wrote them a letter at that time, telling them what a great idea it was. Yet they didn't promote it – even the administration people admitted that.'

L.T. *What are your general thoughts about jazz writing these days? Do you think there's a lot of stereotyped writing going on?*

'Well, I mean – I haven't *heard* that much, but not all the writing I do hear is stereotyped. You know like the writing from here in England: Mike Gibbs – not stereotyped at all. Now in America there's Toshiko Akiyoshi, the Japanese pianist, *she writes*. She's okay – she's not kidding: she's serious. And what about Thad Jones. Phew! He plays too. He has a number now where the band just plays sustained harmony, and he plays – and it's got a Louis Armstrong feel to it. It's beautiful. It thrilled me.'

L.T. *Finally, you don't have a regular band. You record only occasionally. What in fact is your means of livelihood?*
'This last year a man named John Snyder, who ran Horizon Records for A & M, advanced me ten thousand dollars for a solo album. That's helped me – plus the fact that I get social benefit now: 330 dollars a month, which pays the rent. Oh, and I get two thousand a year from BMI.

'See, up until now, economically I've been living a loser's life. I've been an arranger, and you can't get any royalties for arranging. The Columbia President told me the other day that those albums I made with Miles Davis have all gone what they call 'gold' over the years – and yet I only got the original five hundred dollars a piece for the arrangements, after that nothing.'

Gil Evans British Orchestra

A review by Raymond Horricks
of the Royal Festival Hall Concert on 26 August 1983
(by permission of Crescendo International)

The old magician must be quite used to having triumphs by now. But even magic has to be worked at, and on August 26 this latest Evans triumph proved to be yet another example of how the great composer/arranger/leader and pianist gave of himself unstintingly to make his concert an occasion both exciting and thoroughly enjoyable. Any doubt that he isn't the finest orchestral thinker of jazz since Duke Ellington never enters my mind these days. On the other hand, he is very different from Ellington, very individual in all he does, and each time I hear him there are always a few surprises. Sometimes these can be subtle shifts of emphasis within the actual instrumentation, for instance – like only using two trumpets this time, whereas with his previous, all-American band he had the potential of five inside a total personnel of only thirteen players. But whatever and whoever he's leading one can content oneself that he will get the best out of them. And his musicians want to do their best for him. As George Adams put it to me last year: 'When you play with Gil you're aware it's a case of working for a Higher Spirit. But then you also know that his music is going to inspire you to reach out for the higher things . . .'

But then Gil himself is an instinctive picker of men. When one thinks of the legion of big names in jazz who have passed through the ranks of his band, well, it's just staggering. Players as contrasting as Budd Johnson and Ron Carter, Hannibal (Marvin) Peterson and Lew Soloff; and now in 1983 his English ensemble. Gil first formed the Gil Evans Orchestra made up entirely of English musicians for a short tour back in March; and immediately before its apotheosis at the Festival Hall there had been a series of nights at Ronnie Scott's. Even so, it all came off so well the players sounded as if they'd been with him for years. I suspect that, in fact, most of them had – *mentally*, that is. However, the real point I'm making here is: over and above their solo talents, there was a cohesiveness which would never have come about without total dedication. With Gil at the helm these weren't just Englishmen playing together but jazzmen of international stature.

As usual with Gil, he didn't make any chit-chat with the audience. And this gave the set a remarkable continuity. Just a short piano figure between the numbers served as a signal to the musicians – then they were off into the next number. It also made for good internal climaxes and outstanding variations in dynamics, with a piece like, say, Monk's *Friday The Thirteenth* appearing to ebb and flow very much as the sea does; but always vital and never lazily, because the pulsation was there too.

Fine solos abounded, although again with their lengths and approach disciplined by Gil's sure grasp of form and the necessary requirements of impact within any given number. John Surman played as well as I can ever remember, including one 'cadenza' series of variations on baritone which rightly attracted some of the best applause of the evening. Don Weller's big, booting tenor sound was also much in evidence, while there were sparkling contributions from Henry Lowther on trumpet and Ray Russell. I was particularly struck too by Chris Hunter's invention on *Angel*. This Jimi Hendrix number nearly always gets an airing at Evans concerts, always featuring the alto saxophone and, of course, on Evans' own records has come to be associated with Dave Sanborn. However, for this occasion Gil deliberately picked up the tempo somewhat, so enabling Chris Hunter to fashion a new approach to the melody line. It became, in effect, a totally different composition.

Finally, I hardly need to remind anyone except a newcomer to jazz how splendidly drummer John Marshall can fire the rhythm section of a band such as this. Except that there *isn't* another band such as this. How can there be when the brain behind it is unique? There are other good bands, but they have to do their outlays of talent via alternative methods.

Overall this was the best concert of music I've attended at the Festival Hall since February 25, 1978. Funny to have to add that that was a Gil Evans concert too!

The man remains undeterred though. The Orchestra Called Gil Evans lives. Or, as its long-time lead trumpet Ernie Royal put it, 'Gil makes a map, he has a point to go to; there are no detours or things like that. So it comes out to a happy ending.' Royal was a player who had seen it all; having played lead with Lionel Hampton, Basie, Ellington, Woody Herman, Oliver Nelson and Quincy Jones before becoming the most in-demand studio lead on the new York scene. But he had been Evans' regular lead for twenty years and would always try to put off other work to be with him: regardless of the financial loss this sometimes meant. 'He's one of the real innovators,' he insisted. 'He's a very individual man; he thinks out just about everything he's gonna do beforehand, and it manages to come out the way he wants it to. He's very realistic and very honest about his music; he appreciates the guys, and they appreciate him. They really have respect for him, as he has for his fellows.'

Mount Felix, April 1983

Gil Evans

A SELECTIVE DISCOGRAPHY

I have based my selections on records generally available at the time of going to press and further listening suggestions follow the main discography. The following abbreviations have been used (arr) arrangement; (as) alto sax; (b) bass; (bars) baritone sax; (cl) clarinet; (d) drums; (fl) flute; (frh) french horn; (g) guitar; (p) piano; (sop) soprano sax; (tb) trombone; (tp) trumpet; (ts) tenor sax; (tu) tuba; any other instruments are given in full. Only records issued in (Eu) Europe and (Am) United States of America are noted except for some later recordings issued only in (J) Japan. Recording location, (NYC) New York City; (NJ) New Jersey; all other locations given in full.

TONY MIDDLETON *London, February 1984*

Gil Evans

MILES DAVIS with orchestra under the direction of GIL EVANS:

Bernie Glow, Ernie Royal, Louis Mucci, Taft Jordan, John Carisi (tp); Frank Rehak, Jimmy Cleveland, Joe Bennett (tb); Tommy Mitchell (bass,tb); Willie Ruff, Tony Miranda (frh); Bill Barber (tu); Lee Konitz (as); Romeo Penque, Sid Cooper (woodwinds); Danny Bank (bass cl); Paul Chambers (b); Art Taylor (d); Miles Davis (flugel horn); Gil Evans (arr). *NYC. May 6, 1957.*

CO57917	THE MAIDS OF CADIZ	Columbia(Am)CL1041, CBS(Eu)62496
CO57918	THE DUKE	Columbia(Am)CL1041, CBS(Eu)62496

MILES DAVIS with orchestra under the direction of GIL EVANS:

Bernie Glow, Ernie Royal, Louis Mucci, Taft Jordan, John Carisi (tp); Frank Rehak, Jimmy Cleveland, Joe Bennett (tb); Tommy Mitchell (bass,tb); Willie Ruff, Tony Miranda (frh); Bill Barber (tu); Lee Konitz (as); Romeo Penque, Sid Cooper (woodwinds); Danny Bank (bass cl); Paul Chambers (b); Art Taylor (d); Miles Davis (flugel horn); Gil Evans (arr).*NYC. May 10, 1957*

CO57933	MY SHIP	Columbia(Am)CL1041, CBS(Eu)62496
CO57934	MILES AHEAD	Columbia(Am)CL1041, CBS(Eu)62496

MILES DAVIS with orchestra under the direction of GIL EVANS:

Bernie Glow, Ernie Royal, Louis Mucci, Taft Jordan, John Carisi (tp); Frank Rehak, Jimmy Cleveland, Joe Bennett (tb); Tommy Mitchell (bass tb); Willie

A SELECTIVE DISCOGRAPHY

Ruff, Tony Miranda (frh); Bill Barber (tu); Lee Konitz (as); Romeo Penque, Sid Cooper (woodwinds); Danny Bank (bass cl); Paul Chambers (b); Art Taylor (d); Miles Davis (flugel horn); Gil Evans (arr). *NYC, May 23, 1957*

CO58017	NEW RHUMBA	Columbia(Am)CL1041, CBS(Eu)62496
CO58018	BLUES FOR PABLO	Columbia(Am)CL1041, CBS(Eu)62496
CO58019	SPRINGSVILLE	Columbia(Am)CL1041, CBS(Eu)62496

MILES DAVIS with orchestra under the direction of GIL EVANS:

Bernie Glow, Ernie Royal, Louis Mucci, Taft Jordan, John Carisi (tp); Frank Rehak, Jimmy Cleveland, Joe Bennett (tb); Tommy Mitchell (bass tb); Willie Ruff, Tony Miranda (frh); Bill Barber (tu); Lee Konitz (as); Romeo Penque, Sid Cooper, (woodwinds); Danny Bank (bass cl); Paul Chambers (b); Art Taylor (d); Miles Davis (flugel horn); Gil Evans (arr). *NYC. May 27, 1957*

CO58171	I DON'T WANNA BE KISSED	Columbia(Am)CL1041, CBS(Eu)62496
CO58172	THE MEANING OF THE BLUES	Columbia(Am)CL1041, CBS(Eu)62496
CO58173	LAMENT	Columbia(Am)CL1041, CBS(Eu)62496

Note: on one or more of the above dates Jim Buffington (frh) and Eddie Caine (woodwinds) replace Tony Miranda and Sid Cooper.

A SELECTIVE DISCOGRAPHY

GIL EVANS AND TEN:

John Carisi, Jake Koven (tp); Jimmy Cleveland (tb); Bart Varsalona (bass tb); Willie Ruff (frh); Lee Konitz (as); Steve Lacey (sop); Dave Kurtzer (bassoon); Paul Chambers (b); Jo Jones (d); Gil Evans (p,arr). *NJ, September 6, 1957*

| 1346 | REMEMBER | Prestige(Am)7120 |

GIL EVANS AND TEN:

Louis Mucci,Jake Koven (tp); Jimmy Cleveland (tb); Bart Varsalona (bass tb); Willie Ruff (frh); Lee Konitz (as); Steve Lacey (sop); Dave Kurtzer (bassoon); Paul Chambers (b); Nick Stabulas (d); Gil Evans (p,arr). *NYC. September 27, 1957.*

1347	ELLA SPEED	Prestige(Am)7120
1352	NOBODY'S HEART	Prestige(Am)7120
1353	IF YOU COULD SEE ME NOW	Prestige(Am)7120

GIL EVANS AND TEN:

Louis Mucci(tp); Jake Koven (tp); Jimmy Cleveland (tb); Bart Varsalona (bass tb); Willie Ruff (frh); Lee Konitz (as); Steve Lacey (sop); Dave Kurtzer (bassoon); Paul Chambers (b); Nick Stabulas (d); Gil Evans (p,arr). *NYC, October 10, 1957*

1354	BIG STUFF	Prestige(Am)7120
1355	JUST ONE OF THOSE THINGS	Prestige(Am)7120
1356	JAMBANGLE	Prestige(Am)7120

‾‾‾‾‾‾‾‾ Gil Evans ‾‾‾‾‾‾‾‾

A SELECTIVE DISCOGRAPHY

GIL EVANS AND HIS ORCHESTRA:

Louis Mucci, Johnny Coles, Ernie Royal (tp); Frank Rehak, Joe Bennett (tb); Tommy Mitchell (bass tb); Julius Watkins (frh); Harvey Phillips (tu); Cannonball Adderley (as); Jerry Safino (bass cl,fl,piccolo); Chuck Wayne (g); Paul Chambers (b); Art Blakey (d); Gil Evans (p,arr). *NYC, April 9, 1958*

ST LOUIS BLUES	Blue Note(Am) LA461H2
KING PORTER STOMP	Blue Note(Am) LA461H2
'ROUND MIDNIGHT	Blue Note(Am) LA461H2
LESTER LEAPS IN	Blue Note(Am) LA461H2

GIL EVANS AND HIS ORCHESTRA:

Louis Mucci, Johnny Coles, Ernie Royal (tp); Frank Rehak, Joe Bennett (tb); Tommy Mitchell (bass tb); Julius Watkins (frh); Bill Barber (tu); Cannonball Adderley (as); Phil Bodner (bass, cl, fl, piccolo); Chuck Wayne (g); Paul Chambers (b); Philly Joe Jones (d); Gil Evans (p,arr). *NYC, May 2, 1958*

WILLOW TREE	Blue Note(am) LA461H2

GIL EVANS AND HIS ORCHESTRA:

Louis Mucci, Johnny Coles, Ernie Royal (tp); Frank Rehak, Joe Bennett (tb); Tommy Mitchell (bass tb); Julius Watkins(frh); Bill Barber (tu); Cannonball Adderley (as); Phil Bodner (bass cl,fl,piccolo); Chuck Wayne (g); Paul

Gil Evans

A SELECTIVE DISCOGRAPHY

Chambers (b); Art Blakey (d); Gil Evans (p,arr). *NYC, Way 21, 1958*

STRUTTIN' WITH SOME BARBECUE	Blue Note(Am) LA461H2

GIL EVANS AND HIS ORCHESTRA:

Louis Mucci, Johnny Coles, Clyde Reasinger (tp); Frank Rehak, Joe Bennett (tb); Tommy Mitchell (bass tb); Julius Watkins (frh); Bill Barber (tu); Cannonball Adderley (as); Phil Bodner (bass cl,fl,piccolo); Chuck Wayne (g); Paul Chambers (b); Art Blakey (d); Gil Evans (p,arr). *NYC, May 26, 1958*

MANTECA!	Blue Note(Am) LA461H2
BIRD FEATHERS	Blue Notes(Am) LA461H2

MILES DAVIS with orchestra under the direction of GIL EVANS:

Louis Mucci, Ernie Royal, Johnny Coles, Bernie Glow (tp); Jimmy Cleveland, Joe Bennett, Frank Rehak (tb); Dick Hixon (bass tb); Willie Ruff, Julius Watkins, Gunther Schuller (frh); Bill Barber (tu); Cannonball Adderley (as); Phil Bodner, Romeo Penque (fl); Danny Bank (bass cl); Paul Chambers (b); Philly Joe Jones (d); Gill Evans (arr); Miles Davis (tp-1, flugel horn -2). *NYC, July 22, 1958*.

C061300	MY MAN'S GONE NOW – 2	Columbia(Am)PC8085, CBS(Eu)32188
C061301	GONE, GONE, GONE – 2	Columbia(Am)PC8085, CBS(Eu)32188
C061302	GONE – 2	Columbia(Am)PC8085, CBS(Eu)32188

Gil Evans

A SELECTIVE DISCOGRAPHY

MILES DAVIS with orchestra under the direction of GIL EVANS:

Louis Mucci, Ernie Royal, Johnny Coles, Bernie Glow (tp); Jimmy Cleveland, Joe Bennett, Frank Rehak (tb); Dick Hixon (bass tb); Willie Ruff, Julius Watkins, Gunther Schuller (frh); Bill Barber (tu); Cannonball Adderley (as); Phil Bodner, Romeo Penque (fl);Danny Bank (bass cl) Paul Chambers (b); Jimmy Cobb (d); Gil Evans (arr); Miles Davis (tp-1, flugel horn-2). *NYC, July 29, 1958*

C061359	HERE COMES DE HONEYMAN – 1	Columbia(Am)PC8085, CBS(Eu)32188
C061360	BESS, YOU IS MY WOMAN NOW – 2	Columbia(Am)PC8085, CBS(Eu)32188
C061361	IT AIN'T NECESSARILY SO – 2	Columbia(Am)PC8085, CBS(Eu)32188
C061362	FISHERMAN, STRAWBERRY AND DEVIL CRAB – 2	Columbia(Am)PC8085, CBS(Eu)32188

MILES DAVIS with orchestra under the direction of GIL EVANS:

Louis Mucci, Ernie Royal, Johnny Coles, Bernie Glow (tp); Jimmy Cleveland, Joe Bennett, Frank Rehak (tb); Dick Hixon (bass tb); Willie Ruff, Julius Watkins, Gunther Schuller (frh); Bill Barber (tu); Cannonball Adderley (as); Jerome Richardson, Romeo Penque (fl); Danny Bank (bass cl); Paul Chambers (b); Jimmy Cobb (d); Gil Evans (arr); Miles Davis (tp-1, flugel horn-2). *NYC. August 4, 1958*

C061366	PRAYER – 2	Columbia(Am)PC8085, CBS(Eu)32188
C061367	BESS, OH WHERE'S MY BESS – 2	Columbia(Am)PC8085, CBS(Eu)32188
C061368	THE BUZZARD SONG – 2	Columbia(Am)PC8085, CBS(Eu)32188

Gil Evans

MILES DAVIS with orchestra under the direction of GIL EVANS:

Louis Mucci, Ernie Royal, Johnny Coles, Bernie Glow, (tp); Jimmy Cleveland, Joe Bennett, Frank Rehak, (tb); Dick Hixon (bass tb); Willie Ruff, Julius Watkins, Gunther Schuller (frh); Bill Barber (tu); Cannonball Adderley (as); Jerome Richardson, Romeo Penque (fl); Danny Bank (bass cl); Paul Chambers (b); Jimmy Cobb (d); Gil Evans (arr); Miles Davis (tp-1, flugel horn-2). *NYC, August 18, 1958*

C061421	SUMMERTIME – 1	Columbia(Am)PC8085, CBS(Eu)32188
C061422	THERE'S A BOAT THAT'S LEAVING SOON – 2	Columbia(Am)PC8085, CBS(Eu)32188
C061423	I LOVES YOU PORGY – 1	Columbia(Am)PC8085, CBS(Eu)32188

GIL EVANS AND HIS ORCHESTRA:

Louis Mucci, Johnny Coles, Allen Smith (tp); Bill Elton, Curtis Fuller, Dick Lieb (tb); Bill Barber (tu); Steve Lacey (sop); Al Block (woodwind); Chuck Wayne (g); Dick Carter (b); Dennis Charles (d); Gil Evans (p,arr). *NYC, ? early? 1959.*

DAVENPORT BLUES	Blue Note(Am) LA461H2
STRAIGHT, NO CHASER	Blue Note(Am) LA461H2
DJANGO	Blue Note(Am) LA461H2

_____ Gil Evans _____

A SELECTIVE DISCOGRAPHY

GIL EVANS AND HIS ORCHESTRA:

Louis Mucci, Johnny Coles, Danny Styles (tp); Jimmy Cleveland, Rod Levitt (tb); Bill Barber (tu); Earl Chapin (frh); Steve Lacey (sop); Ed Caine (woodwinds); Bud Johnson (cl,ts); Ray Crawford (g); Tommy Potter (b); Elvin Jones (d); Gil Evans (p,arr). *NYC, February 5, 1959*

CHANT OF THE WEED	Blue Note(Am) LA461H2
BALLAD OF THE SAD YOUNG MEN	Blue Note(Am) LA461H2
JOY SPRING	Blue Note(Am) LA461H2
THEME (La Nevada)	Blue Note(Am) LA461H2

MILES DAVIS with orchestra arranged and conducted by GIL EVANS:

Bernie Glow, Ernie Royal, Louis Mucci, Taft Jordan (tp); Frank Rehak, Dick Hixon (tb); John Barrows, Jim Buffington, Earl Chapin (frh); Jay McAllister (tu); Al Block, Ed Caine (flu); Harold Feldman (oboe,cl); Danny Bank (bass cl); Janet Putman (harp); Paul Chambers (b); Jimmy Cobb (d); Elvin Jones (percussion); Gil Evans (arr); Miles Davis (tp-1, flugel horn-2). *NYC, November 20, 1959*

C063971	CONCIERTO DE ARANJUEZ – 1,2	Columbia(Am)PC8271, CBS(Eu)32023

Gil Evans

A SELECTIVE DISCOGRAPHY

MILES DAVIS with orchestra arranged and conducted by GIL EVANS:

Bernie Glow, Ernie Royal, Johnny Coles, (tp); Frank Rehak, Dick Hixon (tb); Joe Singer, Tony Miranda (frh); Bill Barber (tu); Romeo Penque (woodwinds); Jackie Knitzer (bassoon); Al Block (flu); Harold Feldman (oboe,cl); Danny Bank (bass cl); Janet Putman (harp); Paul Chambers (b); Jimmy Cobb (d); Elvin Jones (percussion); Gil Evans (arr); Miles Davis (tp-1, flugel horn-2). *NYC, March 10, 1960*

C064558	THE PAN PIPER – 1	Columbia(Am)PC8271, CBS(Eu)32023

MILES DAVIS with orchestra arranged and conducted by GIL EVANS:

Bernie Glow, Ernie Royal, Louis Mucci, Johnny Coles (tp); Frank Rehak, Dick Hixon, (tb); Joe Singer, Tony Miranda (frh); Bill Barber (tu); Romeo Penque (woodwinds); Jackie Knitzer (basoon); Al Block (flu); Harold Feldman (oboe,cl); Danny Bank (bass cl); Janet Putman (harp); Paul Chambers(b); Jimmy Cobb (d); Elvin Jones (percussion); Gil Evans (arr); Miles Davis (tp-1, flugel horn-2). *NYC, March 11, 1960*

C064560	SOLEA – 1	Columbia(Am)PC8271, CBS(Eu)32023
C064561	WILL O' THE WISP – 1	Columbia(Am)PC8271, CBS(Eu)32023
C064562	SAETA – 1	Columbia(Am)PC8271, CBS(Eu)32023

Gil Evans

A SELECTIVE DISCOGRAPHY

GIL EVANS AND HIS ORCHESTRA:

Johnny Coles, Phil Sunkle (tp); Jimmy Knepper, Keg Johnson (tb); Tony
Studd (bass tb); Bill Barber (tu); Ray Beckenstein (as,fl,piccolo); Bud Johnson
(ts,sop); Bob Tricarico (bassoon,fl,piccolo); Ray Crawford(g); Ron Carter (b);
Charlie Persip, Elvin Jones (percussion); Gil Evans (p,arr). *NYC, ? 1960.*

LA NEVADA	Impulse(Am)A54, Jasmine(Eu)JA552
BILBAO SONG	Impulse(Am)A54, Jasmine(Eu)JA552

GIL EVANS AND HIS ORCHESTRA:

Johnny Coles, Phil Sunkle (tp); Jimmy Knepper, Keg Johnson (tb); Tony
Studd (bass tb); Bill Barber (tu); Ed Caine (as,fl,piccolo); Bud Johnson (ts,sop);
Bob Tricarico (bassoon,fl,piccolo); Ray Crawford (g); Ron Carter (b); Charlie
Persip, Elvin Jones (percussion); Gil Evans (p,arr). *NYC. ? 1960.*

SUNKEN TREASURE	Impulse(Am)A54, Jasmine(Eu)JA552
STRATUSPHUNK	Impulse(Am)A54, Jasmine(Eu)JA552
WHERE FLAMINGOS FLY	Impulse(Am)A54, Jasmine(Eu)JA552

Note: no firm recording date/s for the above titles are known.

Gil Evans

A SELECTIVE DISCOGRAPHY

MILES DAVIS QUINTET with GIL EVANS AND HIS ORCHESTRA:

Quintet: Miles Davis (tp); Hank Mobley (ts)-1; Wynton Kelly (p)-2; Paul Chambers (b); Jimmy Cobb (d). Orchestra: Bernie Glow, Ernie Royal, Louis Mucci, Johnny Coles (tp); Frank Rehak, Dick Hixon, Jimmy Knepper (tb); Julius Watkins, Paul Ingraham, Bob Swisshelm (frh); Bill Barber (tu); Jerome Richardson, Romeo Penque, Eddie Caine, Bob Tricario, Danny Bank (reeds, woodwinds); Janet Putman (harp); Bobby Rosengarden (percussion); Gil Evans (arr). *Carnegie Hall, NYC. May 19, 1961*

C069842	SO WHAT -1,2	Columbia(Am)PC8612, CBS(Eu)85554
C069843	SPRING IS HERE -2	Columbia(Am)PC8612, CBS(Eu)85554
C069847	THE MEANING OF THE BLUES/ LAMENT/NEW RHUMBA	Columbia(Am)PC8612, CBS(Eu)85554

Note: further titles from the above concert on PC8612 and 85554 are by the Miles Davis Quintet.

MILES DAVIS with ORCHESTRA CONDUCTED BY GIL EVANS:

Ernie Royal, Bernie Glow, Louis Mucci, Johnny Coles (tp); Frank Rehak, Dick Hixon, Jimmy Knepper (tb); Julius Watkins, Paul Ingraham, Bob Swisshelm (frh); Bill Barber (tu); Steve Lacy (sop); Jerome Richardson, Eddie Caine, Romeo Penque, Danny Bank (reeds,woodwind); Janet Putman (harp); Paul Chambers (b); Jimmy Cobb (d); Bobby Rosengarden (percussion); Gil Evans (arr); Miles Davis (tp-1, flugel horn-2). *NYC. July 27, 1962*

Gil Evans

A SELECTIVE DISCOGRAPHY

C075683	CORCOVADO -1,2	Columbia(Am)PC8906, CBS(Eu)85556
C075257	AOS PES DA CRUZ -2	Columbia(Am)PC8906, CBS(Eu)85556

MILES DAVIS with ORCHESTRA CONDUCTED BY GIL EVANS;

Ernie Royal, Bernie Glow, Louis Mucci, Johnny Coles (tp); Frank Rehak, Dick Hixon, Jimmy Knepper (tb); Julius Watkins, Paul Ingraham, Bob Swisshelm (frh); Bill Barber (tu); Steve Lacy (sop); Jerome Richardson, Eddie Caine, Romeo Penque, Danny Bank (reeds,woodwind); Janet Putman (harp); Paul Chambers (b); Jimmy Cobb (d); Bobby Rosengarden (percussion); Gil Evans (arr); Miles Davis (tp-1, flugel horn-2). *NYC. August 13, 1962*

C075678	SONG No.1 -1	Columbia(Am)PC8906, CBS(Eu)85556
C075837	WAIT TILL YOU SEE HER -1	Columbia(Am)PC8906, CBS(Eu)85556

MILES DAVIS with ORCHESTRA CONDUCTED BY GIL EVANS:

Ernie Royal, Bernie Glow, Louis Mucci, Johnny Coles (tp); Frank Rehak, Dick Hixon, Jimmy Knepper (tb); Julius Watkins, Jimmy Buffington, John Burrows (frh); Bill Barber (tu); Steve Lacy (sop); Jerome Richardson, Eddie Caine, Romeo Penque, Danny Bank (reeds,woodwind); Janet Putman (harp); Paul Chambers (b); Jimmy Cobb (d); Bob Tricarico (reeds,woodwind) Gil Evans (arr); Miles Davis (tp-1, flugel horn-2). *NYC. November 6, 1962.*

Gil Evans

A SELECTIVE DISCOGRAPHY

C077119	ONCE UPON A SUMMERTIME -1	Columbia(Am)PC8906, CBS(Eu)85556
C077120	SONG No.2. -1	Columbia(Am)PC8906, CBS(Eu)85556

GIL EVANS AND HIS ORCHESTRA:

Jimmy Cleveland (tb); Gil Cohen, Don Corado, Julius Watkins (frh); Steve Lacey (sop); Al Block (fl); Eric Dolphy (fl,bass cl); Bob Tricarico (ts); Margaret Ross (harp); Barry Gailbraith (g); Paul Chambers, Ben Tucker, Richard Davis (b); Elvin Jones (d); Gil Evans (p,arr). *NYC. September 1963*

FLUTE SONG   Verve V6-8555

GIL EVANS AND HIS ORCHESTRA;

Johnny Coles, Louis Mucci; Ernie Royal (tp); Jimmy Cleveland, Tony Studd (tb); Jimmy Buffington, Bob Northern (frh); Steve Lacey (sop); Eric Dolphy (as,fl,bass cl); Bob Tricarico (ts); Jerome Richardson (fl,bars); Paul Chambers, Richard Davis, Milt Hinton (b); Osie Johnson (d); Gil Evans (p,arr). *NYC. September 1963*

EL TOREADOR   Verve V6-8555

Gil Evans

A SELECTIVE DISCOGRAPHY

GIL EVANS AND HIS ORCHESTRA

2 (tp); 2 (tb); frh; tu; Phil Woods (as); 3 (woodwinds); violin; vibes, Kenny Burrell (g); Ron Carter (b); Elvin Jones (d); Gil Evans (p,arr). *NYC. ? Autumn 1963?*

SPOONFUL	Verve V6-8838
CONCORDE	Verve V6-8838

GIL EVANS QUARTET:

Tony Studd (tb); Gil Evans (p,arr); Paul Chambers (b); Clifford Jarvis (d). *NYC. ? 1963*

BLUES IN ORBIT	Verve V6-8838
ISABEL	Verve V6-8838

GIL EVANS AND HIS ORCHESTRA:

Johnny Coles, Bernie Glow (tp); Jimmy Cleveland, Tony Studd (tb); Ray Alonge (frh); Bill Barber (tu); Steve Lacy (sop); Eric Dolphy (as,fl,bass cl); Bob Tricarico, Garvin Bushell (reeds,fl); Kenny Burrell (g); Ron Carter, Paul Chambers (b); Elvin Jones (d); Gil Evans (p,arr). *NYC. April 6, 1964.*

HOTEL ME	Verve V6-8555
LAS VEGAS TANGO	Verve V6-8555

Gil Evans

A SELECTIVE DISCOGRAPHY

GIL EVANS AND HIS ORCHESTRA:

Frank Rehak (tb); Ray Alonge, Julius Watkins (frh); Bill Barber (tu); Al Block, Andy Fitzgerald, George Marge, Bob Tricarico (fl,bass fl,english horn,bassoon); Wayne Shorter (ts); Bob Maxwell (harp); Gary Peacock (b); Elvin Jones (d); Gil Evans (p,arr). *NYC. July 9, 1964.*

THE BARBARA SONG	Verve V6-8555
BARRACUDA	Verve V6-8838

KENNY BURRELL arranged and conducted by GIL EVANS:

Johnny Coles or Louis Mucci (tp); Jimmy Cleveland, Jimmy Knepper (tb); Ray Alonge or Julius Watkins (frh); John Barber (tu); Lee Konitz (as); Steve Lacy (sop); Bob Tricarico (ts,fl,bassoon); Ray Beckenstein (alto fl,fl,bass cl); Andy Fitzgerald (english horn,fl); Ron Carter (b); Elvin Jones, Charlie Persip (percussion); Gil Evans (arr); Kenny Burrell (g). *NJ. December 14 or 15, 1964.*

LOTUS LAND	Verve(Am)56 8612, (Eu)2304158
MOON AND SAND	Verve(Am)56 8612, (Eu)2304158
LOIE	Verve(Am)56 8612, (Eu)2304158
GREENSLEEVES	Verve(Am)56 8612, (Eu)2304158
LAST NIGHT WHEN WE WERE YOUNG	Verve(Am)56 8612, (Eu)2304158

Note: other titles from the above issue are by Kenny Burrell.

A SELECTIVE DISCOGRAPHY

GIL EVANS ORCHESTRA:

Snooky Young, Mike Lawrence (tp); Jimmy Cleveland, Jimmy Knepper (tb);
Julius Watkins (frh); Howard Johnson (tu); Hubert Laws (fl); Billy Harper (ts);
Gene Bianco (harp); Joe Beck (g); Herb Bushler (b); Elvin Jones (d); Sue Evans
(percussion); Gil Evans (p,electric p,arr). *NYC. 1969.*

GENERAL ASSEMBLY	Enja(Eu)3069
PROCLAMATION	Enja(Eu)3069
LOVE IN THE OPEN	Enja(Eu)3069
SPACED	Enja(Eu)3069
VARIATION ON THE MISERY	Enja(Eu)3069
SO LONG	Enja(Eu)3069

GIL EVANS AND HIS ORCHESTRA:

Ernie Royal, Johnny Coles (tp); Jimmy Cleveland, Garnett Brown (tb); Julius
Watkins, Ray Alonge (frh); George Marge (fl,sop); Billy Harper (fl,ts); Joe Beck
(guitar); Howard Johnson (tuba,bass); Herb Bushler (b); Alphonse Mouzon
(d); Donald McDonald (percussion); Gil Evans (p,electric p,arr). *NYC 1971*

THOROUGHBRED	Enja(Eu)3069
BLUES IN ORBIT	Enja(Eu)3069

GIL EVANS ORCHESTRA

Johnny Coles (tp); Billy Harper (ts); Howard Johnson (tu,bars^); Harry
Lookofsky (tenor-violin); Joe Beck (g,mandolin*); Herb Bushler (b); Don
Preston (synthesiser); Lennie White (dr); Sue Evans (percussion*,Marimba);
Airto Moreira, Flora Purim (percussion**,vcl**); Gil Evans (elp,tank-p**
,arr,cond). *NYC. 1971*

EL MATADOR*	Artists House AH14
ZEE ZEE	Artists House AH14

*Notes: **These were overdubbed in 'El Matador'.*

Gil Evans

GIL EVANS ORCHESTRA

Johnny Coles, Hannibal Marvin Peterson, Stan Shafran (tp); Jimmy Knepper (tb); Billy Harper (ts,chime*); Howard Johnson (bars,flh***); Trevor Koehler (as,bars); Bruce Johnson (g); Richard Davis (bass); Bill Quinze (b); Phil Davis, Don Preston (synthesiser); Bruce Ditmas (d); Gil Evans (p,elp**,arr,cond). *NYC. 1971*

LOVE YOUR LOVE	Artists House AH14
HOTEL ME** (Jelly Rolls)	Artists House AH14
WHERE FLAMINGOS FLY***	Artists House AH14

*Notes: *This was overdubbed in 'Love Your Love'.*

GIL EVANS ORCHESTRA;

Johnny Coles, Hannibal Marvin Peterson, Stan Shafran (tp); Jimmy Knepper (tb); Billy Harper (ts,chimes*); Howard Johnson (bars,flh***); Trevor Koehler (as,bars); Bruce Johnson (g); Richard Davis (b); Bill Quinze (b); Phil Davis, Don Preston (synthesiser); Bruce Ditmas (d); Airto Moreira, Flora Purim (vcl*), Sue Evans (percussion); Gil Evans (p,elp**,arr,cond). *NYC. 1971*

NAÑA	Artists House AH14

*Notes: *These were overdubbed.*

GIL EVANS:

Tex Allen, Richard Williams (tp); Howard Johnson (tu,bars,flugel horn);

Gil Evans

Joseph Daley (tb,tu); Peter Levin, Sharon Freeman (frh); David Sanborn (as); Billy Harper (ts,fl); Trevor Koehler (bars,sop,fl); David Horowitz (synthesizers); Ted Dunbar (guitar); Herb Bushler (b); Bruce Ditmas (d); Sue Evans (percussion); Gil Evans (p,electric p,arr). *NYC. May 30, 1973*

27215	THOROUGHBRED	Atlantic(Am)AT90048
27216	ELEVEN	Atlantic(Am)AT90048
27217	CRY OF HUNGER	Atlantic (Am)AT90048
27218	BLUES IN ORBIT	Atlantic(Am)AT90048
27219	SUMMERTIME	Atlantic(Am)AT90048

GIL EVANS:

Hannibal Marvin Peterson, Richard Williams (tp); Howard Johnson (tu,bars,flugel horn); Joseph Daley (tb,tu); Peter Levin, Sharon Freeman (frh); David Sanborn (as); Bill Harper (ts,fl); Trevor Koehler (bars,sop,fl); David Horowitz (synthesizers); Ted Dunbar (guitar); Herb Bushler (b); Bruce Ditmas (d); Sue Evans (percussion); Gil Evans (p,electric p,arr). *NYC. June 3, 1973.*

27226	ZEE ZEE	Atlantic(Am)AT90048

Note: May 30th titles recorded at Trinity Church, New York. June 3 title recorded at Philharmonic Hall, New York.

THE GIL EVANS ORCHESTRA:

Hannibal Marvin Peterson (tp,vocal); Lew Soloff (tp); Howard Johnson (tu,bass cl,b,bugle,arr-1); Tom Malone (tb,fl,b,synthesizer,arr-2); Peter Gordon (frh); Pete Levin (frh,synthesizer); David Sanborn (as,fl,sop); Billy

A SELECTIVE DISCOGRAPHY

Harper (ts,fl); Trevor Koehler (ts,bars,fl,arr-3); David Horowitz (electric p, synthsizer, arr-4); John Abercrombie, Ryo Kawasaki (electric g); Keith Loving (g); Michael Moore, Don Pate (b); Bruce Ditmas (d); Sue Evans (conga drums); Warren Smith (chimes,vibes,percussion,arr-5); Gil Evans (p,arr). *NYC. June 11,12 & 13, 1974*

ANGEL -2	RCA(Am)CPL1-0677
CROSSTOWN TRAFFIC -2, vHMP; LITTLE MISS LOVER -2	RCA(Am)CPL1-0677
CASTLES MADE OF SAND; FOXY LADY -5	RCA(Am)CPL1-0677
UP FROM THE SKIES	RCA(Am)CPL1-0677
1983; A MERMAN I SHOULD TURN TO BE -4	RCA(Am)CPL1-0677
VOODOO CHILE -1	RCA(Am)CPL1-0677
GYPSY EYES -3	RCA(Am)CPL1-0677

GIL EVANS AND HIS ORCHESTRA:

Hannibal Marvin Peterson (tp,koto,vocal); Lew Soloff, Ernie Royal (tp,fl); John Clark, Peter Gordon (frh); Joe Daley (tb); Bob Stewart (tu); Howard Johnson (tu,bars,bass cl); David Sanborn (as,sop,fl); George Adams, Billy Harper (ts,fl); Tom Malone (tb,tu,piccolo,synthesizer); David Horowitz (organ,synthesizer); Pete Levin (frh,organ,synthesizer); Paul Metzke (synthesizer); Ryo Kawasaki (guitar); Herb Bushler (b); Joe Gallivan (bells,steel g, drum synthesizer); Bruce Ditmas (tabla,cuica,percussion); Sue Evans (timpani,congas,cowbell,celeste); Warren Smith (marimba,chimes,gongs, vibes,tuned cl); Tony Williams (d); Gil Evans (p,electric p,celeste,arr). *NYC 1975*

KING PORTER STOMP	RCA(Am)APL1-1057

Gil Evans

MAKES HER MOVE	RCA(Am)APL1-1057
LITTLE WING vHMP	RCA(Am)APL1-1057
ANITA'S DANCE	RCA(Am)APL1-1057

GIL EVANS AND HIS ORCHESTRA:

Hannibal Marvin Peterson (tp,koto,vocal); Lew Soloff, Ernie Royal (tp,fl); John Clark, Peter Gordon (frh); Joe Daley (tu); Howard Johnson (tu,bars,bass cl); David Sanborn (as,sop,fl); George Adams, Billy Harper (ts,fl); Tom Malone (tb,tu,piccolo,synthesizer); David Horowitz (organ,synthesizer); Pete Levin (frh,organ,synthesizer); Paul Metzke (synthesizer); Ryo Kawasaki (guitar); Herb Bushler (b); Joe Gallivan (bells, steel g, drum synthesizer); Bruce Ditmas (tabla,cuica,percussion); Sue Evans (timpani,congas,cowbell,celeste); Warren Smith (marimba,chimes, vibes, tuned d); Tony Williams (d); Gil Evans (p,electric p, celeste,arr). *NYC 1975*

THE MEANING OF THE BLUES	RCA(Am)APL1-1057
AFTERMATH THE FOURTH	RCA(Am)APL1-1057
MOVEMENT CHILDREN OF	
THE FIRE	

GIL EVANS AND HIS ORCHESTRA:

Hannibal Marvin Peterson, (tp,koto,vocal); Lew Soloff, Ernie Royal (tp,flugel horn); John Clark, Peter Gordon (frh); Joe Daley (tb); Bob Stewart (tu); Howard Johnson (tu,bars,bass cl); David Sanborn (as,sop,fl); George Adams, Billy Harper (ts,fl); Tom Malone (tb,tu,piccolo,synthesizer); David Horowitz (organ,synthesizer); Pete Levin (frh,organ,synthesizer); Paul Metzke (b); Ryo Kawasaki (guitar); Herb Bushler (b); Joe Gallivan (bells,steel g, drum synthesizer); Bruce Ditmas (tabla,cuica,percussion); Sue Evans (timpani, congas, cowbell,celeste); Warren Smith (marimba,chimes,gong,vibes tuned d);

Gil Evans

A SELECTIVE DISCOGRAPHY

Tony Williams (d); Gil Evans (p,electric p,celeste,arr). *NYC. 1975.*

THERE COMES A TIME vHMP   RCA(Am)APL1-1057

GIL EVANS:

Hannibal Marvin Peterson, Ernie Royal (tp); Lew Soloff (tp,piccolo tp); Jimmy Knepper (tb); John Clark (frh); Howard Johnson, Bob Stewart (tu); Arthur Blythe, David Sanborn (as); George Adams (ts); Pete Levin (clavinet, synthesizer); Keith Loving (g); Steve Neil (b); Sue Evans (d); Gil Evans (p,arr). *NYC. May 13, 1977.*

PRIESTESS	Antilles(Am)AN1010
SHORT VISIT	Antilles(Am)AN1010
LUNAR ECLIPSE	Antilles(Am)AN1010
ORANGE WAS THE COLOUR OF HER DRESS, THEN BLUE SILK	Antilles(Am)AN1010

Note: the above recording was from a concert at St. Georges Church, New York.

GIL EVANS;

Hannibal Marvin Peterson (tp,chimes); Ernie Royal (tp,flugel horn); Lew Soloff (tp,piccolo tp); Bob Stewart (flugel horn, tu); John Clark (frh,g); Arthur Blythe (as,sop); David Sanborn (as,sop,fl,sopranino); George Adams (ts,sop, bass cl,alto fl); Pete Levin (clavinet, mini moog); Masabumi Kikuchi (keyboards); Herb Bushler (bass); Sue Evans (percussion); Howard Johnson (arr)-1; Tom Malone (arr)-2; Gil Evans (p, electric p,arr). *London. February 25, 1978*

Gil Evans

A SELECTIVE DISCOGRAPHY

ANGEL -2	RCA(Eu)PL25209
PARABOLA	RCA(Eu)PL25209
ORANGE WAS THE COLOUR OF HER DRESS, THEN BLUE SILK	RCA(Eu)PL25209
STONE FREE	RCA(Eu)PL25209
FUGUE FROM CONCORD	RCA(Eu)PL25209
BLUES INC. MEDLEY: Cheryl; Birdhead;Relaxing at Camarillo	RCA(Eu)PL25209
EPILOGUE	RCA(Eu)PL25209
RHYTHM-A-NING	Mole Jazz(Eu)Mole3
UP FROM THE SKIES	Mole Jazz(Eu)Mole3
VARIATION ON THE MISERY	Mole Jazz(Eu)Mole3
VOODOO CHILE -1	Mole Jazz(Eu)Mole3

GIL EVANS:

Lou Soloff (tp); Earl McIntyre (tb); Steve Lacy (sop); Arthur Blythe (as,sop); Pete Levin (keyboards); Don Pate (b); Noel McGhee (d); Gil Evans (p, electric p,arr). *Rome. July 29, 1978*

WALTZ	Horo(Eu)HDP31/2
UP FROM THE SKIES	Horo(Eu)HDP31/2
PARABOLA	Horo(Eu)HDP31/2
STONE FREE	Horo(Eu)HDP31/2
VARIATION (on the misery)	Horo(Eu)HDP31/2

THE GIL EVANS ORCHESTRA:

Terumasa Hino (tp); Lew Soloff (tp,piccolo tp); Gerry Niewood (as,fl,sop);

Gil Evans

A SELECTIVE DISCOGRAPHY

George Adams (ts,fl,percussion); Bob Stewart (tu); Pete Levin (synthesizer); Don Pate (b); Robert Crowder (d); Gil Evans (electric p). *West Germany, October 1978.*

DR JECKYLL (Jackie)	Circle(Eu)RK101978/13,Inner City(Am)1110
THE MEANING OF THE BLUES	Circle(Eu)RK101978/13,Inner City(Am)1110
LITTLE WING	Circle(Eu)RK101978/13,Inner City(Am)1110

GIL EVANS:

Hannibal Marvin Peterson, John Faddis, Lew Soloff (tp); George Lewis (tb); Dave Bargeron (tb,tu); John Clark (frh); Arthur Blythe (as,sop); Hamiet Bluiett (bars,alto fl); Masabumi Kikuchi (polyphonic synthesizer, bass synthesizer, mono synthesizer, organ); Pete Levin (clarinet, mini-moog, four voice synthesizer); Tim Landers (b); Billy Cobham (d); Alyrio Lima (percussion); Gil Evans (electric p, arr). *NYC. February 8 & 9, 1980.*

ANITA'S DANCE	Trio(J)PAP9233
JELLY ROLLS	Trio(J)PAP9233
ALYRIO	Trio(J)PAP9233
VARIATIONS ON THE MISERY	Trio(J)PAP9233
GONE, GONE, GONE	Trio(J)PAP9233
UP FROM THE SKIES	Trio(J)PAP9233
COPENHAGEN SIGHT	Trio(J)PAP25016
ZEE ZEE	Trio(J)PAP25016

Gil Evans

SIRHAN'S BLUES	Trio(J)PAP25016
STONE FREE	Trio(J)PAP25016
ORANGE WAS THE COLOUR OF	Trio(J)PAP25016
HER DRESS, THEN BLUE SILK	

Note: the above titles are from concerts at the Public Theatre, New York. Both issues titled "Live at the Public Theatre (New York 1980)"

GIL EVANS:

Guy Barker, Miles Evans, Henry Lowther (tp); Malcolm Griffiths (tb); Rick Taylor (tb,bass tb); Chris Hunter (as,sop,fl); Don Weller (ts,sop); Stan Sulzman (ts,sop,fl); John Surman (bars,sop,bass cl,syntheziser); John Taylor (keyboards); Ray Russell (g); Mo Foster (b); John Marshall (d); Gil Evans (p,electric p,arr). *West Yorkshire, England. March 18, 1983*

HOTEL ME	Mole Jazz(Eu)Mole 8
FRIDAY THE 13th	Mole Jazz(Eu)Mole 8
LONDON	Mole Jazz(Eu)Mole 8
LITTLE WING	Mole Jazz(Eu)Mole 8

Note: above titles recorded at St Georges Hall, Bradford, England.

Gil Evans

A SELECTIVE DISCOGRAPHY

Further listening suggestions:–

CLAUDE THORNHILL ORCHESTRA:

Gil Evans arrangements, on Columbia, and transcription recordings, plus radio broadcast reissues.

MILES DAVIS ORCHESTRA:

Gil Evans arrangements on radio broadcast reissues but most important, Capitol recordings, BIRTH OF THE COOL. Capitol (Eu) CAPS 1024

CHARLIE PARKER ORCHESTRA:

Gil Evans arrangements – three titles Verve 1953.

More examples of Gil Evans' work, slightly outside the scope of this discography, are as follows.

Billy Butterfield Orchestra – London – early 50's.

Al Martino – Capitol – early 50's.

Teddy Charles Tentet – Atlantic – 1956

Johnny Mathis – Columbia – 1956

Hal McKusick – RCA – 1956

Helen Merrill – EmArcy – 1956

Marcy Lutes – Decca – mid 50's

Lucy Reed – Decca – 1957

Don Elliott – ABC Paramount – 1957

Astrud Gilberto – Verve – mid 60's

Japanese artists from early 70's – issued only in Japan

Pearl Bailey – Columbia – early 50's

Bibliography

Alun Morgan and Raymond Horricks, *Modern Jazz, A Survey Of Developments Since 1939*, Victor Gollancz, London

Ed. Raymond Horricks, *Jazzmen Of Our Time*, Victor Gollancz, London

Ian Carr, *Miles Davis*, Quartet Books, London

Leonard Feather and Ira Gitler', *Encyclopedia Of Jazz In The 'Sixties' And 'Seventies'*, New York, Quartet Books, London

There is no other single book devoted to Gil Evans. In 'Modern Jazz' he is one of several arrangers discussed in the chapter about Miles Davis' 1948/49 band. In 'Jazzmen Of Our Time' there is a complete chapter on him by Charles Fox, ending with the first formation of his own orchestra. In Ian Carr's book he is very well discussed over the period of his association with Miles; the other books contain 'thumbnail' sketches and condensed musical analysis. Meanwhile he has been written intelligently about in certain album notes: by Nat Hentoff ('Sketches Of Spain', CBS); Ed Michel ('New Bottle, Old Wine', Pacific Jazz'); and Dave Gelly ('Gil Evans At The Royal Festival Hall, 1978', RCA). With at least five pieces based on interviews by Les Tomkins in the magazine 'Crescendo International'.